SIXTH EDITION

JAVA™ PROGRAMS TO ACCOMPANY *PROGRAMMING LOGIC AND DESIGN*

BY JO ANN SMITH

COURSE TECHNOLOGY
CENGAGE Learning™

Australia • Brazil • Japan • Korea • Mexico • Singapore • Spain • United Kingdom • United States

COURSE TECHNOLOGY
CENGAGE Learning™

Java Programs to Accompany *Programming Logic and Design*, Sixth Edition
Jo Ann Smith

Executive Editor: Marie Lee

Acquisitions Editor: Amy Jollymore

Senior Product Manager: Alyssa Pratt

Development Editor: Mary Pat Shaffer

Content Project Manager: Jennifer Feltri

Art Director: Marissa Falco

Proofreader: Suzanne Ciccone

Indexer: Sharon Hilgenberg

Compositor: Integra

For product information and technology assistance, contact us at
Cengage Learning Customer & Sales Support, 1-800-354-9706

For permission to use material from this text or product,
submit all requests online at **www.cengage.com/permissions**
Further permissions questions can be e-mailed to
permissionrequest@cengage.com

Library of Congress Control Number: 2010928661

ISBN-13: 978-0-538-74480-5
ISBN-10: 0-538-74480-4

Course Technology
20 Channel Center Street
Boston, MA 02210
USA

Cengage Learning is a leading provider of customized learning solutions with office locations around the globe, including Singapore, the United Kingdom, Australia, Mexico, Brazil, and Japan. Locate your local office at: **international.cengage.com/region**

Cengage Learning products are represented in Canada by Nelson Education, Ltd.

For your lifelong learning solutions, visit **course.cengage.com**
Visit our corporate Web site at **cengage.com**.

Some of the product names and company names used in this book have been used for identification purposes only and may be trademarks or registered trademarks of their respective manufacturers and sellers.

Any fictional data related to persons or companies or URLs used throughout this book is intended for instructional purposes only. At the time this book was printed, any such data was fictional and not belonging to any real persons or companies.

Course Technology, a part of Cengage Learning, reserves the right to revise this publication and make changes from time to time in its content without notice.

The programs in this book are for instructional purposes only.
They have been tested with care, but are not guaranteed for any particular intent beyond educational purposes. The author and the publisher do not offer any warranties or representations, nor do they accept any liabilities with respect to the programs.

Printed in the United States of America
1 2 3 4 5 6 7 14 13 12 11 10

Brief Contents

Contents

CHAPTER 5   Writing Programs Using Loops **75**

CHAPTER 6   Using Arrays in Java Programs **101**

Preface

Java Programs to Accompany Programming Logic and Design, Sixth Edition (also known as *Java PAL*) is designed to provide students with an opportunity to write Java programs as part of an introductory programming logic course. It accompanies the student's primary text, *Programming Logic and Design, Sixth Edition*, by Joyce Farrell. This textbook assumes no programming language experience and provides the beginning programmer with a guide to writing structured programs and simple object-oriented programs using introductory elements of the popular Java programming language. It is not intended as a textbook for a course in Java programming. The writing is nontechnical and emphasizes good programming practices. The examples do not assume mathematical background beyond high school math. Additionally, the examples illustrate one or two major points; they do not contain so many features that students become lost following irrelevant and extraneous details.

The examples in *Java PAL, Sixth Edition* are often examples presented in the primary textbook, *Programming Logic and Design, Sixth Edition*. The following table shows the correlation between topics in the two books.

Java PAL, Sixth Edition	Programming Logic and Design, Sixth Edition
Chapter 1: An Introduction to Java and the Java Programming Environment	Chapter 1: An Overview of Computers and Logic
Chapter 2: Variables, Constants, Operators, and Writing Programs Using Sequential Statements	Chapter 2: Working with Data, Creating Modules, and Designing High-Quality Programs Chapter 3: Understanding Structure
Chapter 3: Writing Structured Java Programs	Chapter 2: Working with Data, Creating Modules, and Designing High-Quality Programs Chapter 3: Understanding Structure

(continues)

x

(continued)

Java PAL, Sixth Edition	Programming Logic and Design, Sixth Edition
Chapter 4: Writing Programs That Make Decisions	Chapter 4: Making Decisions
Chapter 5: Writing Programs Using Loops	Chapter 5: Looping
Chapter 6: Using Arrays in Java Programs	Chapter 6: Arrays
Chapter 7: File Handling and Applications	Chapter 7: File Handling and Applications
Chapter 8: Advanced Array Techniques	Chapter 8: Advanced Array Concepts, Indexed Files, and Linked Lists
Chapter 9: Advanced Modularization Techniques	Chapter 9: Advanced Modularization Techniques
Chapter 10: Additional Topics	Chapter 10: Object-Oriented Programming
	Chapter 11: More Object-Oriented Programming Concepts
	Chapter 12: Event Driven GUI Programming, Multithreading, and Animation

Organization and Coverage

Java Programs to Accompany Programming Logic and Design, Sixth Edition provides students with a review of the programming concepts they are introduced to in their primary textbook. It also shows them how to use Java to transform their program logic and design into working programs. Chapter 1 introduces the structure of a Java program, how to compile and run a Java program, and introductory object-oriented concepts. Chapter 2 discusses Java's data types, variables, constants, arithmetic and assignment operators, and using sequential statements to write a complete Java program. In Chapter 3, students learn how to transform pseudocode and flowcharts into Java programs. Chapters 4 and 5 introduce students to writing Java programs that make decisions and programs that use looping constructs. Students learn to use Java to develop more sophisticated programs that include using arrays, control breaks, and file input and output in Chapters 6 and 7. In Chapter 8, students learn about sorting data items in an array and using multidimensional arrays. Passing parameters to procedures is introduced in Chapter 9. Lastly, in Chapter 10, students use Java to write programs that include programmer-defined classes. This last chapter also gives students some experience in creating a graphical user interface (GUI).

This book combines text explanation of concepts and syntax along with pseudocode and actual Java code examples to provide students with the knowledge they need to implement their logic and program designs using the Java programming language. This book is written in a modular format and provides paper-and-pencil exercises as well as lab exercises after each major topic is introduced. The exercises provide students with experience in reading and writing Java code as well as modifying and debugging existing code. In the labs, students are asked to complete partially prewritten Java programs. Using partially prewritten programs allows students to focus on individual concepts rather than an entire program. The labs also allow students to see their programs execute.

Java PAL, Sixth Edition is unique because:

- It is written and designed to correspond to the topics in the primary textbook, *Programming Language and Design, Sixth Edition*.

- The examples are everyday examples; no special knowledge of mathematics, accounting, or other disciplines is assumed.

- It introduces students to introductory elements of the Java programming language rather than overwhelming beginning programmers with more detail than they are prepared to use or understand.

- Text explanations are interspersed with pseudocode from the primary book, thus reinforcing the importance of programming logic.

- Complex programs are built through the use of complete examples. Students see how an application is built from start to finish instead of studying only segments of programs.

Features of the Text

Every chapter in this book includes the following features. These features are both conducive to learning in the classroom and enable students to learn the material at their own pace.

- Objectives: Each chapter begins with a list of objectives so the student knows the topics that will be presented in the chapter. In addition to providing a quick reference to topics covered, this feature provides a useful study aid.

- Figures and illustrations: This book has plenty of visuals, which provide the reader with a more complete learning experience, rather than one that involves simply studying text.

- Notes: These brief notes provide additional information—for example, a common error to watch out for.

- Exercises: Each section of each chapter includes meaningful paper-and-pencil exercises that allow students to practice the skills and concepts they are learning in the section.

- Labs: Each section of each chapter includes meaningful lab work that allows students to write and execute programs that implement their logic and program design.

Acknowledgments

I would like to thank all the people who helped to make this book possible, especially Mary Pat Shaffer, Development Editor, whose expertise and attention to detail have made this a better textbook. She also provided encouragement, patience, humor, and flexibility when needed. Thanks also to Alyssa Pratt, Senior Product Manager, and Amy Jollymore, Acquisitions Editor, for their help and encouragement. I am grateful to Jennifer Feltri, Content Project Manager, and Vidya Muralidharan, of Integra Software Services, for overseeing the production of the printed book. It is a pleasure to work with so many fine people who are dedicated to producing quality instructional materials.

I am dedicating this book to my husband, Ray, whose patience and encouragement allow me to pursue projects such as this book.

Jo Ann Smith

Read This Before You Begin

To the User

Data Files

To complete most of the lab exercises, you will need data files that have been created for this book. Your instructor can provide the data files. You can also obtain the files electronically from the Course Technology Web site by connecting to *www.course.com*, and then searching for this book title.

You can use a computer in your school lab or your own computer to complete the lab exercises in this book.

Solutions

Solutions to the Exercises and Labs are provided to instructors on the Course Technology Web site at *www.course.com*. The solutions are password protected.

Using Your Own Computer

To use your own computer to complete the material in this book, your computer must be included in the list of Java-supported systems. To view this list, go to *http://java.sun.com/javase/6/webnotes/install/system-configurations.html*.

This book was written using Microsoft Windows Vista and Quality Assurance tested using Microsoft Windows Vista and Windows 7.

Downloading the Java Standard Edition Development Kit (JDK6) for the Windows Platform

To download JDK6, go to the download Web site at *http://java.sun.com/javase/downloads/index.jsp.*

- Click the **Download JDK** button in the Java Platform, Standard Edition, JDK 6 Update XX section of the Web page. The "XX" represents digits that change as Sun releases new downloads. You may have to scroll down to be able to see the Download JDK button.

- On the next screen, select your operating system platform (e.g., Windows) from the drop-down list and then click **Download**. By clicking Download, you accept the terms and conditions of the Java SE Development Kit 6uxx License Agreement.

- Click **Skip this Step** on the Login for Download window.

- When the next window appears, you are asked if you want to save the download file. Click **Save File** (Firefox) or **Save** (Internet Explorer).

- In the Save As dialog box (Internet Explorer) or the "Enter name of file to save to …" window (Firefox), specify your Desktop as the location in which to save the downloaded file, then click **Save**. (In Firefox, the file may automatically be downloaded to your Downloads folder.) You will be downloading the file named jdk-6uxx-windows-i586.exe. The "xx" represents digits that change as Sun releases new downloads. Depending on the speed of your connection, this could take some time.

- When the download is complete, note that the size of the file (in bytes) is provided on the download screen. Check that the file you downloaded is the same size. This means you have downloaded the full, uncorrupt file.

Installing the Java Standard Edition Development Kit (JDK6)

- On your Desktop, double-click **jdk-6uXX-windows-i586-p-iftw. exe**. This starts the installation program.

- Next,
  - In Vista: You may have to click the **Continue** button on the User Account Control dialog box.
  - In XP: Click **Run** on the Open File Security Warning dialog box.
  - In Windows 7: You may have to click the **Yes** button in the User Account Control dialog box.

- Read the Software License Agreement, and then click **Accept**.

- In the Custom Setup dialog box, select Development Tools if it is not already selected. At the bottom left, you see "Install to." By default, the files will be installed in the C:\Program Files\Java\ jdk1.6.0_XX\ folder. You should not change this location unless you have a good reason to do so.

- Click the **Next** button.

- After a few moments, the Destination Folder dialog box is displayed, showing you the folder where Java will be installed. You should not change this location unless you have a good reason to do so. Click the **Next** button.

- The Java Setup program now installs the Java SE Development Kit 6. Files are copied to the appropriate folders. This takes a few minutes. When the setup is complete, you see the message "Java SE Development Kit 6 Update XX Successfully Installed" in the dialog box. Click **Finish** to complete the setup.

- When the installation is complete, you can delete the downloaded file, jdk-6uxx-windows-i586.exe to recover disk space.

Updating Your PATH Environment Variable

Setting the PATH variable allows you to use the compiler (javac) and bytecode interpreter (java) without having to specify the full path for the command.

To set the PATH permanently in Windows 7:

1. Click the **Start** button in the lower left corner of your Desktop.

2. Select **Control Panel**, click **System and Security**, and then click **System**.

3. Select the **Advanced system settings** link. Click **Yes**.

4. In the System Properties dialog box, select the **Advanced** tab, if necessary, and then click the **Environment Variables** button.

5. Select **PATH** or **Path** in the User variables or System variables section, click **Edit**, and then edit the PATH variable by adding the following to the end of the current PATH:

    ;C:\Program Files\Java\jdk1.6.0_XX\bin

Note that it is important to include the semicolon (;) at the beginning of the path, preceding C:\. Replace the "XX" with the update number you have downloaded. A typical PATH might look like this:

C:\Windows;C:\Windows\System32;C:\Program Files\Java\jdk1.6.0_19\bin

6. When you are finished editing the PATH variable, click **OK**.

7. Click **OK** on the Environment Variables dialog box.

8. Click **OK** on the System Properties dialog box.

9. Close the System window.

To set the PATH permanently in Windows Vista:

1. Click the **Start** button in the lower left corner of your Desktop.

2. Select **Control Panel** and then select **Classic View**, if necessary.

3. Double-click **System**.

4. Select the **Advanced system settings** link. Click **Continue**, if necessary.

5. In the System Properties dialog box, select the **Advanced** tab, if necessary, and then click the **Environment Variables** button.

6. Select **PATH** or **Path** in the User variables or System variables section, click **Edit**, and then edit the PATH variable by adding the following to the end of the current PATH:

;C:\Program Files\Java\jdk1.6.0_XX\bin

Note that it is important to include the semicolon (;) at the beginning of the path, preceding C:\. Replace the "XX" with the update number you have downloaded. Add the path to the end of the current PATH. A typical PATH might look like this:

C:\Windows;C:\Windows\System32;C:\Program Files\Java\jdk1.6.0_19\bin

7. When you are finished editing the PATH variable, click **OK**.

8. Click **OK** on the Environment Variables dialog box.

9. Click **OK** on the System Properties dialog box.

10. Close the System window.

To set the PATH permanently in Windows XP:

1. Click the **Start** button in the lower left corner of your Desktop.

2. Select **Control Panel** and then double-click **System**.

3. In the System Properties dialog box, select the **Advanced** tab, and then click the **Environment Variables** button.

4. Select **PATH** or **Path** in the User variables or System variables section, click **Edit**, and then edit the PATH variable by adding the following to the end of the current PATH:

   ;C:\Program Files\Java\jdk1.6.0_XX\bin

   Note that it is important to include the semicolon (;) at the beginning of the path, preceding C:\. Replace the "XX" with the update number you have downloaded. A typical PATH might look like this:

   C:\Windows;C:\Windows\System32;C:\Program Files\Java\ jdk1.6.0_19\bin

5. When you are finished editing the PATH variable, click **OK**.

6. Click **OK** on the Environment Variables dialog box.

7. Click **OK** on the System Properties dialog box.

8. Close the System window.

Capitalization does not matter when you are setting the PATH variable. The PATH is a series of folders separated by semicolons (;). Windows searches for programs in the PATH folders in order, from left to right.

To find out the current value of your PATH, at the prompt in a Command Prompt window, type: **path**.

Updating Your CLASSPATH Environment Variable

Setting the CLASSPATH variable allows you to execute Java programs without having to specify the full path for the program. You may not have to update the CLASSPATH environment variable unless instructed to do so by your professor.

If you do want to update the CLASSPATH environment variable, follow the steps you used to edit the PATH variable up to the point of editing the PATH variable. Then do the following:

1. Select **CLASSPATH** or **classpath** in the User variables or System variables section, click **Edit**, and then edit the CLASSPATH variable by adding a semicolon (;) followed by a period (.) to the end of the "CLASSPATH". A typical CLASSPATH might look like this:

   C:\Program Files\Java\jdk1.6.0_19\bin;.

2. When you are finished editing the CLASSPATH variable, click **OK**.

3. Click **OK** on the Environment Variables dialog box.

4. Click **OK** on the System Properties dialog box.

5. Close the System window.

If you don't have a CLASSPATH environment variable, click the **New** button, enter CLASSPATH for the variable name and a period (.) for the variable value.

Capitalization does not matter when you are setting the CLASSPATH variable. The CLASSPATH is a series of folders separated by semicolons (;). Java searches for classes in the CLASSPATH folders in order, from left to right.

To find out the current value of your CLASSPATH, at the prompt in a Command Prompt window, type: **set classpath**.

To the Instructor

To complete some of the Exercises and Labs in this book, your students must use the data files provided with this book. These files are available on the Course Technology Web site at *www.course. com*. Follow the instructions in the Help file to copy the data files to your server or stand-alone computer. You can view the Help file using a text editor such as WordPad or Notepad. Once the files are copied, you may instruct your students to copy the files to their own computers or workstations.

Course Technology Data Files

You are granted a license to copy the data files to any computer or computer network used by individuals who have purchased this book.

An Introduction to Java and the Java Programming Environment

After studying this chapter, you will be able to:

◎ Discuss the Java programming language and its history

◎ Recognize the three types of Java programs

◎ Explain introductory concepts and terminology used in object-oriented programming

◎ Download the Java Standard Edition Development Kit (JDK)

◎ Recognize the structure of a Java program

◎ Complete the Java development cycle, which includes creating a source code file, compiling the source code, and executing a Java program

You should do the exercises and labs in this chapter only after you have finished Chapter 1 of your book, *Programming Logic and Design, Sixth Edition*, by Joyce Farrell. This chapter introduces the Java programming language and its history. It explains some introductory object-oriented concepts, describes the process of compiling and executing a Java program, and explains how to download the Java Standard Edition Development Kit (JDK). You begin writing Java programs in Chapter 2 of this book.

The Java Programming Language

The Java programming language was developed by Dr. James Gosling and introduced by Sun Microsystems in late 1995. It became very popular in a short period of time, mostly due to the rising popularity of the World Wide Web. Java is a programming language that can be used to create interactive Web pages and to write Web-based applications that run on Web servers. **Web servers** are the computers that "serve up" content when you request to view Web pages. An online bookstore and an online course registration system are examples of **Web-based applications**. Java is also used to develop **stand-alone enterprise applications** (programs that help manage data and run a business) and applications for cell phones and personal digital assistants.

What makes Java especially useful is that it is an object-oriented programming language. The term **object-oriented** encompasses a number of concepts explained later in this chapter and throughout this book. For now, all you need to know is that an object-oriented programming language is modular in nature, allowing the programmer to build a program from reusable parts of programs called classes, objects, and methods.

 Many of the terms used to describe the JDK may be unfamiliar to you. Don't worry about that right now. By the time you finish with this chapter, you will understand this new terminology and you will even be using some of the tools that are part of the JDK.

The Java programming language is just one part of an object-oriented system called the Java Standard Edition Development Kit (JDK). You will use the JDK when you write, compile, and execute Java programs in this book. The JDK includes many reusable parts of programs, called **packages**. Programmers use these packages to simplify their programming tasks. The JDK also includes development tools used by program developers. Examples of development tools include the **compiler** (javac) and the **bytecode interpreter** (java) that you will use later in this chapter.

Three Types of Java Programs

Java programs can be written as applications, servlets, or applets. An **application** is a stand-alone program. A **servlet** is a Java program that runs on a Web server or application server and provides server-side processing, such as accessing a database and handling e-commerce transactions. An **applet** is a Java program that is executed and viewed in a browser such as Mozilla Firefox or Internet Explorer. In this book, you will write applications, which means you will be writing stand-alone Java programs.

An Introduction to Object-Oriented Terminology

You must understand a few object-oriented concepts to be successful at reading and working with Java programs in this book. Note, however, that you will not learn enough to make you a Java programmer. You will have to take additional courses in Java to become a Java programmer. This book teaches you only the basics.

To fully understand the term *object-oriented*, you need to know a little about procedural programming. Procedural programming is a style of programming that is older than object-oriented programming. **Procedural programs** consist of statements that the computer runs or **executes**. Many of the statements make calls (a request to run or execute) to groups of other statements that are known as procedures, modules, methods, or subroutines. These programs are known as "procedural" because they perform a sequence of procedures. Procedural programming focuses on writing code that takes some data (for example, some sales figures), performs a specific task using the data (for example, adding up the sales figures), and then produces output (for example, a sales report). When people who use procedural programs (the **users**) decide that they want their programs to do something slightly different, a programmer must revise the program code, taking great care not to introduce errors into the logic of the program.

Today, we need computer programs that are flexible and easy to revise. Object-oriented programming languages, including Java, were introduced to meet this need. In object-oriented programming, the programmer can focus on the data that he or she wants to manipulate, rather than the individual lines of code required to manipulate that data (although those individual lines still must be written eventually). An **object-oriented program** is made up of a collection of interacting objects.

An **object** represents something in the real world, such as a car, an employee, or an item in an inventory. An object includes (or **encapsulates**) both the data related to the object and the tasks you can perform on that data. The term **behavior** is sometimes used to refer to the tasks you can perform on an object's data. For example, the data for an inventory object might include a list of inventory items, the number of each item in stock, the number of days each item has been in stock, and so on. The behaviors of the inventory object might include calculations that add up the total number of items in stock and calculations that determine the average amount of time each item remains in inventory.

In object-oriented programming, the data items within an object are known collectively as the object's **attributes**. You can think of an attribute as one of the characteristics of an object, such as its shape, its color, or its name. The tasks the object performs on that data are known as the object's **methods**. (You can also think of a method as an object's behavior.) Because methods are built into objects, when you create a Java program, you don't always have to write multiple lines of code telling the program exactly how to manipulate the object's data. Instead, you can write a shorter line of code, known as a **call**, that passes a message to the method indicating that you need it to do something.

For example, you can display dialog boxes, scroll bars, and buttons for a user of your program to type in or click on simply by sending a message to an existing object. At other times, you will be responsible for creating your own classes and writing the code for the methods that are part of that class. Whether you use existing, prewritten classes or create your own classes, one of your main jobs as a Java programmer is to communicate with the various objects in a program (and the methods of those objects) by passing messages. Individual objects in a program can also pass messages to other objects.

When Java programmers begin to write a program, they must begin by creating a class. A **class** can be thought of as a template for a group of similar objects. In a class, the programmer specifies the data (attributes) and behaviors (methods) for all objects that belong to that class. An object is sometimes referred to as an **instance** of a class, and the process of creating an object is referred to as **instantiation**.

To understand the terms *class*, *instance*, and *instantiation*, it's helpful to think of them in terms of a real-world example—baking a chocolate cake. The recipe is similar to a class, and an actual cake is an object. If you wanted to, you could create many chocolate cakes that are all based on the same recipe. For example, your mother's birthday cake, your sister's anniversary cake, and the cake for your neighborhood bake sale all might be based on a single recipe that contains the same data (ingredients) and methods (instructions). In object-oriented programming, you can create as many objects as you need in your program from the same class.

Downloading the Java Standard Edition Development Kit (JDK)

All the examples in this book were created using the Java Standard Edition Development Kit (JDK 6 Update 14). You can get your own copy of the JDK and install it on your computer at home, or your school may have the JDK installed in your lab.

To get your own copy, go to the Java SE Web site at *http://java.sun.com/javase/downloads/index.jsp*. Click the Download button in the JDK 6 Update "X" section. The "X" represents a digit that changes as Sun releases new downloads. (You might see a section labeled "JDK 6 Update 18," or something similar.) Then follow the directions for downloading and installing the correct version of the software for your computer's operating system. Refer to the "Read This Before You Begin" section at the front of this book, or ask your instructor, if you have questions regarding this process.

The Structure of a Java Program

When a programmer learns a new programming language, the first program he or she traditionally writes is a Hello World program—a program that displays the message "Hello World" on the screen. Creating this simple program illustrates that the language is capable of instructing the computer to communicate with the outside world. The Java version of the Hello World program is shown in Figure 1-1.

```
public class HelloWorld
{
    public static void main(String args[])
    {
        System.out.println("Hello World.");
    }
}
```

Figure 1-1   Hello World program

At this point, you're not expected to understand all the code in Figure 1-1. Just notice that the code begins with the word public, followed by the word class. Both public and class are special words, known as **keywords**, which are reserved by Java to have a special meaning. The keyword public indicates that the class you are about to create should be available when the program executes. The class keyword tells the Java compiler that you are beginning the creation of a class and that what follows is part of that class. The name of the

In Java, it is a convention to begin class names with a capital letter. If a class name is made up of two or more words, the first letter of each word in the name is typically capitalized, with no spaces between the words.

You can tell main() is a method because of the parentheses; all Java method names are followed by parentheses.

class is up to you; however, the name should be meaningful, and it cannot contain any spaces. Because this program is written to display the words "Hello World" on the user's screen, it makes sense to name the class HelloWorld.

The opening curly brace ({) on the second line of Figure 1-1 marks the beginning of the class named HelloWorld. The closing curly brace (}) on the last line of Figure 1-1 marks the end of the class.

Below the opening curly brace you see the method named main().

This is a special method in a Java program; the main() method is the first method that executes when any program runs. The programs in the first eight chapters of this book will include only the main() method. In later chapters you will be able to include additional methods.

The first part of any method is its **header**. In Figure 1-1, the header for the main() method begins with the public keyword, followed by the static keyword, followed by the void keyword, followed by the method name, which is main(). The public keyword makes this method available to a user who wants to run the program. At this point, you don't have to understand the keyword static. Just keep in mind that it's necessary to make the Hello World program work.

To understand the keyword void you need to know that methods often create some kind of output (for example, the result of a calculation), which can then be used elsewhere in the program. Another way to say this is that methods sometimes return a value. In Figure 1-1, the keyword void indicates that the main() method does not return anything. You will learn more about methods returning values in Chapter 9 of this book.

When we use the main() method in Java code, we always insert String args[] within the parentheses following the word main, like this: main(String args[]). This makes it possible to pass some arguments, or values, to the main() method. You will learn more about passing arguments to methods in Chapter 9. For now, you will have to include String args[] in the parentheses without understanding why. Remember that Java is a complex programming language; you will have much more to learn about it after you finish this course in order to become a Java programmer.

The line following the header for main() begins with another opening curly brace. This curly brace marks the beginning of the main() method. The closing curly brace on the second-to-last line of Figure 1-1 marks the end of the main() method. All the code within this pair of curly braces executes when the main() method executes. In Figure 1-1, there is only this one line of code between the curly braces:

```
System.out.println("Hello World.");
```

This is the line that causes the words "Hello World." to appear on the user's screen. This line consists of two parts. The first part, `System.out.println();`, prints (that is, displays on the screen) whatever is included within its parentheses. In this example, the parentheses contain the message "Hello World." so that is what will appear on the screen. (The quotation marks will not appear on the screen, but they are necessary to make the program work.) Note that the semicolon that ends the `System.out.println("Hello World.");` statement is required because it tells the compiler that this is the end of the statement.

In the statement `System.out.println("Hello World.");`, `System` is a class, `out` is an object, and `println()` is a method. Java programs frequently use this class-dot-object-dot-method syntax.

Next, you learn about the Java development cycle so that later in this chapter, you can compile the Hello World program and execute it. The Hello World program is saved in a file named `HelloWorld.java` and is included in the student files for this chapter.

The Java Development Cycle

When you finish designing a program and writing the Java code that implements your design, you must compile and execute your program. This three-step process of writing code, compiling code, and executing code is called the Java development cycle. It is illustrated in Figure 1-2.

Let's begin by learning about Step 1, writing the Java source code.

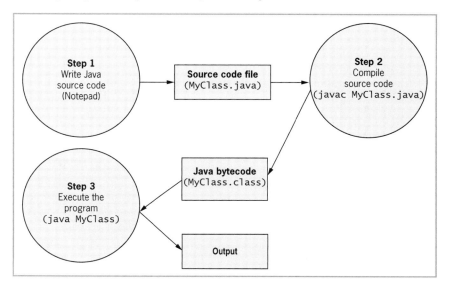

Figure 1-2 The Java development cycle

Writing Java Source Code

As you learned in the previous section, you write a Java program by creating a class and including a method named `main()` in the class. But what do you use to write the program, and where do you save it?

To write a Java program, you use a text editor, such as the Windows text editor, Notepad. You can use any text editor, but the steps in this book assume you are using Notepad. To start Notepad, click the **Start** button, point to **Programs** or **All Programs**, click **Accessories**, and then click **Notepad**. Once Notepad starts, you simply type in your Java source code. **Source code** is the name used for the statements that make up a Java program. For example, the code shown earlier in Figure 1-1 is source code.

 The name of the file and the name of the class must match exactly, including upper-case and lowercase letters. It would not be correct to name the source code file `helloworld.java` because the lowercase "h" and lowercase "w" do not match the uppercase "H" and uppercase "W" in the class name.

When you save the file that contains the source code, it is important to name the file using the same name as the class and to add the extension `.java`. For the Hello World program, the class is named `HelloWorld`; therefore, the name of the source code file must be `HelloWorld.java`. Of course, it is also important to remember the location of the folder in which you choose to save your source code file.

You move on to Step 2 of the Java development cycle after saving your source code file. In Step 2, you compile the source code.

Compiling a Java Program

As you learned earlier in this chapter, the JDK contains several utility programs. One of these utilities is the Java compiler, named `javac`. The `javac` compiler is responsible for taking your source code and transforming it into bytecode. **Bytecode** is intermediate, machine-independent code. **Intermediate** means that the code is between source code and machine code. **Machine code** is made up of 1s and 0s, which a computer needs to execute a program. The Java compiler automatically saves the intermediate bytecode in a file. This file has the same name as the source code file, but it has a `.class` extension rather than a `.java` extension. The bytecode generated by the compiler is platform independent. This is an important feature of Java. **Platform independence** means that the same Java program can be executed on many different types of computers that run many different operating systems.

The following steps show how to compile a source code file. These steps assume you have already created and saved the HelloWorld.java source code file.

1. Set your PATH environment variable. Refer to "Read This Before You Begin" at the front of this book or ask your instructor for instructions on how to set the PATH environment variable.

2. Set your CLASSPATH environment variable. Refer to the "Read This Before You Begin" section at the beginning of this book for instructions on how to set the CLASSPATH environment variable.

3. Open a Command Prompt window. To do this in Windows XP, click the **Start** button, point to **Programs**, point to **Accessories**, and then click **Command Prompt**. In Vista or Windows 7, click the **Start** button, point to **All Programs**, click **Accessories**, and then click **Command Prompt**. The cursor blinks to the right of the current file path.

4. To compile your source code file, you first have to change to the file path containing your source code file. To do this, type **cd driveletter:\path** where **driveletter** is the drive containing your file, and **path** is the path to the folder containing your file. For example, to open a file stored in a folder named "Testing," which is in turn stored in a folder named "My Program," which is stored on the C: drive, you would type **cd c:\My Program\Testing**. After you type the command, press **Enter**. The cursor now blinks next to the file path for the folder containing your source code file.

5. Type the following command, which uses the Java compiler, javac, to compile the program:

    javac HelloWorld.java

    If there are no syntax errors in your source code, a file named HelloWorld.class is created. You do not see anything special happen. However, the file you just created contains the byte-code for the Hello World program. If there are syntax errors, you will see error messages on the screen. In that case, you need to go back to Notepad to fix the errors, save the source code file again, and recompile until there are no syntax errors remaining. **Syntax errors** tell you what your errors are and where they are located in your source code file.

The PATH environment variable tells your operating system which directories on your system contain commands.

The CLASSPATH environment variable tells your operating system which directories on your system contain resources it needs to run your program.

If you are working in a school computer lab, the first two steps might already have been performed for you.

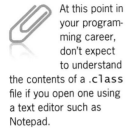

At this point in your programming career, don't expect to understand the contents of a .class file if you open one using a text editor such as Notepad.

6. After the program is compiled, you can use the dir command to display a directory listing to see the file named HelloWorld.class. To execute the dir command, you type dir at the command prompt. For example, if your source code file is located at C:\My Program\Testing, the command prompt and dir command should look like this: **C:\My Program\Testing>dir**. The HelloWorld.class file should be in the same directory as the source code file, HelloWorld.java.

Step 3 in the development cycle is executing the Java program. You'll learn about that next.

Executing a Java Program

As you know, a computer can understand only machine code (1s and 0s), so a Java program must eventually be transformed from bytecode into machine code before it can be executed. The **Java Virtual Machine (JVM)** is an **interpreter** that is responsible for transforming bytecode into machine code and then executing that machine code.

There are many JVMs available from different vendors and written for different purposes. For example, Web browsers, such as Internet Explorer and Mozilla Firefox, contain a JVM. There is a JVM for the Windows operating system, another for the Mac operating system, and yet another for the Linux operating system. You will most likely use the Windows JVM when you execute your Java programs. The name of the JDK utility you use to transform bytecode and execute your Java programs is java.

To execute the Hello World program, do the following:

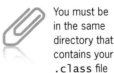

You must be in the same directory that contains your .class file when you execute the program.

1. Open a Command Prompt window. To do this in Windows XP, click the **Start** button, point to **Programs**, point to **Accessories**, and then click **Command Prompt**. In Vista or Windows 7, click the **Start** button, point to **All Programs**, click **Accessories**, and then click **Command Prompt**. Change to the file path containing your source code file, if necessary, and then enter the following command:

```
java HelloWorld
```

2. When the program executes, the words "Hello World." appear in a Command Prompt window.

Figure 1-3 illustrates the steps involved in compiling HelloWorld.java using the javac compiler, executing the dir command to verify that the file HelloWorld.class was created, and executing the Hello World program using the java interpreter.

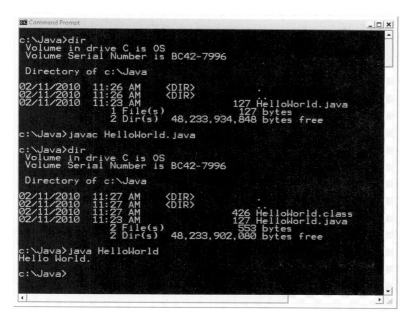

Figure 1-3   Compiling and executing the Hello World program

Exercise 1-1:   Understanding Java Utilities

In this exercise, assume you have written a Java program and stored your source code in a file named MyJavaProgram.java. Then, answer Questions 1–3.

1. What is the name of the class stored in this file?

   _____

2. What command would you use to compile the source code?

   _____

3. What command would you use to execute the program?

   _____

LAB 1.1 Compiling and Executing a Java Program

In this lab, you compile and execute a prewritten Java program, and then answer Questions 1–6.

1. Open the source code file named GoodMorning.java using Notepad or the text editor of your choice.

2. Save this source code file in a directory of your choice, and then change to that directory.

3. Compile the source code file. There should be no syntax errors. Record the command you used to compile the source code file.

   _____

   _____

4. Execute the program. Record the command you used to execute the program, and also record the output of this program.

   _____

   _____

5. Modify the class so that it displays "Good Job!," and then change the class name to GoodJob. Save the file as GoodJob.java. Compile and execute the program.

6. Modify the GoodJob class so that it prints two lines of output. Change the class name to GoodJob2. Add a second output statement that displays "Have a great day." Save the modified file as GoodJob2.java. Compile and execute the program.

CHAPTER 2

Variables, Constants, Operators, and Writing Programs Using Sequential Statements

After studying this chapter, you will be able to:

- ◎ Name variables and use appropriate data types

- ◎ Declare and initialize variables

- ◎ Understand and use unnamed and named constants

- ◎ Use arithmetic operators in expressions

- ◎ Use assignment operators in assignment statements

- ◎ Write Java comments

- ◎ Write programs using sequential statements and interactive input statements

In this chapter, you learn about writing programs that use variables, constants, and arithmetic operators, and that receive interactive input from a user of your programs. We begin by reviewing variables and constants and learning how to use them in a Java program. You should do the exercises and labs in this chapter only after you have finished Chapters 2 and 3 of your book, *Programming Logic and Design, Sixth Edition*, by Joyce Farrell.

Variables

As you know, a **variable** is a named location in the computer's memory whose contents can vary (thus the term *variable*). You use a variable in a program when you need to store values. The values stored in variables often change as a program executes.

In Java, you must declare variables before you can use them in a program. Declaring a variable is a two-part process: first you give the variable a name, and then you specify its data type. You'll learn about data types shortly. But first, we'll focus on the rules for naming variables in Java.

Variable Names

A variable is sometimes referred to as an identifier.

Variable names in Java can consist of letters, numerical digits, a dollar sign, and the underscore character, but they cannot begin with a digit.

You cannot use a Java keyword for a variable name. As you learned in Chapter 1 of this book, a keyword is a word with a special meaning in Java. The following are all examples of legal variable names in Java: my_var, num6, intValue, and firstName. Table 2-1 lists some examples of invalid variable names, and explains why each is invalid.

By convention, variable names in Java begin with a lowercase letter; all other words in the name begin with an uppercase letter—for example, firstName. You cannot include spaces between the words in a variable name.

Name of Variable	Explanation
3wrong	Invalid because it begins with a digit
$don't	Invalid because it contains a single quotation mark
public	Invalid because it is a Java keyword

Table 2-1   Invalid variable names

When naming variables, keep in mind that Java is **case sensitive**—in other words, Java knows the difference between uppercase and lowercase characters. That means value, Value, and VaLuE are three different variable names in Java.

In Java, variable names can be as long as you want. A good rule is to give variables meaningful names that are long enough to describe how the variable is used, but not so long that you make your program hard to read or cause yourself unnecessary typing. For example, a variable named firstName will clearly be used to store someone's first name. The variable name freshmanStudentFirstNam is descriptive but inconveniently long; the variable name fn is too short and not meaningful.

Java Data Types

In addition to specifying a name for a variable, you also need to specify a particular data type for that variable. A variable's **data type** dictates the amount of memory that is allocated for the variable and the type of data that you can store in the variable. There are many different kinds of data types, but in this book we will focus on the most basic kind of data types, known as **primitive data types**. There are eight primitive data types in Java: byte, short, int, long, float, double, char, and boolean. Some of these data types (such as short, int, long, double, and float) are used for variables that will store numeric values, and are referred to as numeric data types. The others have specialized purposes. For example, the boolean data type is used to store a value of either true or false.

You will not use all of Java's primitive data types in the programs you write in this book. Instead, you will focus on two of the numeric data types (int and double). The int data type is used for values that are whole numbers. For example, you could use a variable with the data type int to store someone's age (for example, 25) or the number of students in a class (for example, 35). A variable of the int data type consists of 32 bits (4 bytes) of space in memory. You use the data type double to store a floating-point value (that is, a fractional value), such as the price of an item ($2.95) or a measurement (2.5 feet). A variable of the double data type consists of 64 bits (8 bytes) of space in memory. You will learn about using other data types as you continue to learn more about Java in subsequent courses.

In *Programming Logic and Design, Sixth Edition*, data type num is used to refer to all numeric data types; a distinction is not made between int and double as it is in Java.

The int and double data types will be adequate for all the numeric variables you will use in this book. But what about when you need to store a group of characters (such as a person's name) in a variable? In programming, we refer to a group of one or more characters as a string. An example of a string is the last name "Wallace" or a product type such as a "desk". There is no primitive data type in Java for storing strings; instead, they are stored in an object known as a String object. In addition to working with the int and double data types in this book, you will also work with Strings.

Exercise 2-1: Using Java Variables, Data Types, and Keywords

In this exercise, you use what you have learned about naming Java variables, Java data types, and keywords to answer Questions 1–2.

1. Is each of the following a legal Java variable name? (Answer "yes" or "no.")

myAge	_____	this_is_a_var	_____	NUMBER	_____
yourAge	_____	number	_____	$number	_____
float	_____	1number	_____	intNum	_____
May25	_____	number Two	_____	Number	_____

2. What data type (`int`, `double`, or `String`) is appropriate for storing each of the following values?

   A person's height in inches _____

   The price of a pair of shoes _____

   The name of your pet _____

   The amount of interest on a loan, such as 10% _____

   The number of CDs you own _____

Declaring and Initializing Variables

Now that you understand the rules for naming a variable, and you understand the concept of a data type, you are ready to learn how to declare a variable. In Java, you must declare all variables before you can use them in a program. When you **declare** a variable, you tell the compiler that you are going to use the variable. In the process of declaring a variable, you must specify the variable's name and its data type. Declaring a variable tells the compiler that it needs to reserve a memory location for the variable. A line of code that declares a variable is known as a **variable declaration**. The Java syntax for a variable declaration is as follows:

```
dataType variableName;
```

For example, the declaration statement `int counter;` declares a variable named `counter` of the `int` data type. The compiler reserves the amount of memory space allotted to an `int` variable (32 bits, or 4 bytes) for the variable named `counter`. The compiler then assigns the new variable a specific memory address. In Figure 2-1, the memory address for the variable named `counter` is 1000, although you wouldn't typically know the memory address of the variables included in your Java programs.

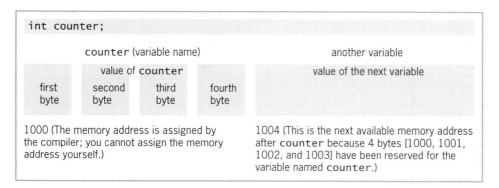

Figure 2-1   Declaration of variable and memory allocation

You can also initialize a Java variable when you declare it. When you **initialize** a Java variable, you give it an initial value. For example, you can assign an initial value of 8 to the `counter` variable when you declare it, as shown in the following code:

```
int counter = 8;
```

You can also declare and initialize variables of data type `double` and `String` variables as shown in the following code:

```
double salary;
double cost = 12.95;
String firstName;
String homeAddress = "123 Main Street";
```

You can declare more than one variable in one statement as long as they have the same data type. For example, the following statement declares two variables, named `counter` and `value`. Both variables are of the `int` data type.

```
int counter, value;
```

Numeric variables are automatically initialized to zero (0), unless you specify a different value.

Exercise 2-2: Declaring and Initializing Java Variables

In this exercise, you use what you have learned about declaring and initializing Java variables to answer Questions 1–2.

1. Write a Java variable declaration for each of the following. Use `int`, `double`, or `String` and choose meaningful variable names.

    Declare a variable to store a product number (1–1000).

    _____

    Declare a variable to store the number of pets in your family.

    _____

Declare a variable to store the price of a pair of boots.

_____

Declare a variable to store the name of your favorite book.

_____

2. Declare and initialize variables to represent the following values. Use int, double, or String and choose meaningful variable names.

One side of a rectangle that is 5.1 inches in length _____
The number of days in November _____
The name of your dog, "Duchess" _____
The number of credit hours you are taking this term

_____

LAB 2.1 Declaring and Initializing Java Variables

In this lab, you declare and initialize variables in a Java program provided with the data files for this book. The program, which is saved in a file named NewAge.java, calculates your age in the year 2040.

1. Open the source code file named NewAge.java using Notepad or the text editor of your choice.

2. Declare an integer variable named newAge.

3. Declare and initialize an integer variable named currentAge. Initialize this variable with your current age.

4. Declare and initialize an integer variable named currentYear. Initialize this variable with the value of the current year. Use four digits for the year.

5. Save this source code file in a directory of your choice, and then make that directory your working directory.

6. Compile the source code file NewAge.java.

7. Execute the program. Record the output of this program.

_____

_____

Constants

As you know, a **constant** is a value that never changes. In Java, you can use both unnamed constants as well as named constants in a program. You'll learn about named constants shortly. But first, we'll focus on unnamed constants.

Unnamed Constants

Computers are able to deal with two basic types of data: text and numeric. When you use a specific numeric value, such as 35, in a program, you write it using the numbers, without quotation marks. A specific numeric value is called a **numeric constant** because it does not change; a 35 always has the value 35. When you use a specific text value, or string of characters, such as "William," you enclose the **string constant** in double quotation marks. Both of the preceding examples, 35 and "William," are examples of **unnamed constants** because they do not have specified names as variables do.

Named Constants

In addition to variables, Java allows you to create named constants. A **named constant** is similar to a variable, except it can be assigned a value only once. You use a named constant when you want to assign a name to a value that will never be changed when a program executes.

By convention, in Java the names of constants are written in all uppercase letters. This makes it easier for you to spot named constants in a long block of code.

To declare a named constant in Java, you use the keyword, final, followed by the data type, followed by the name of the constant. Named constants must be initialized when they are declared, and their contents may not be changed during the execution of the program. For example, the following statement declares an int constant named MAX_STUDENTS and initializes MAX_STUDENTS with the value 35.

```
final int MAX_STUDENTS = 35;
```

Exercise 2-3: Declaring and Initializing Java Constants

In this exercise, you use what you have learned about declaring and initializing Java constants to answer the question.

1. Declare and initialize constants to represent the following values. Use int, double, or String and choose meaningful names.

    The price of a car wash is $14.95._____

    The number of days in November is 30._____

    The name of your dog is "Duchess"._____

    The maximum number of credit hours you may take in a term is 18._____

LAB 2.2   Declaring and Initializing Java Constants

In this lab, you declare and initialize constants in a Java program provided with the data files for this book. The program, which is saved in a file named NewAge2.java, calculates your age in the year 2040.

1. Open the source code file named NewAge2.java using Notepad or the text editor of your choice.

2. Declare a constant named YEAR and initialize YEAR with the value 2040.

3. Edit the following statement so that it uses the constant named YEAR:

```
newAge = currentAge + (2040 - currentYear);
```

4. Edit the following statement so that it uses the constant named YEAR:

```
System.out.println("I will be" + newAge + "in 2040.");
```

5. Save this source code file as NewAge2.java in a directory of your choice, and then make that directory your working directory.

6. Compile the source code file NewAge2.java.

7. Execute the program. Record the output of this program.

_____

_____

Arithmetic and Assignment Operators

After you declare a variable, you can use it in various tasks. For example, you can use variables in simple arithmetic calculations, such as adding, subtracting, and multiplying. You can also perform other kinds of operations with variables, such as comparing one variable to another to determine which is greater.

In order to write Java code that manipulates variables in this way, you need to be familiar with operators. An **operator** is a symbol that tells the computer to perform a mathematical or logical operation. Java has a large assortment of operators. We begin the discussion with a group of operators known as the arithmetic operators.

Arithmetic Operators

Arithmetic operators are the symbols used to perform arithmetic calculations. You are probably already very familiar with the arithmetic operators for addition (+) and subtraction (-). Table 2-2 lists and explains Java's arithmetic operators.

Operator Name and Symbol	Example	Comment
Addition +	`num1 + num2`	
Subtraction -	`num1 - num2`	
Multiplication *	`num1 * num2`	
Division /	`15/2`	Integer division; result is 7; fraction is truncated
	`15.0 / 2.0`	Floating-point division; result is 7.5
	`15.0 / 2`	Floating-point division because one of the operands is a floating-point number; result is 7.5
Modulus %	`hours % 24`	Performs division and finds the remainder; result is 1 if the value of `hours` is 25
Unary plus +	`+num1`	Maintains the value of the expression; if the value of `num1` is 3, then `+num1` is 3
Unary minus -	`-(num1 - num2)`	If value of (`num1 - num2`) is 10, then `-(num1 - num2)` is −10

Table 2-2 Java arithmetic operators

You can combine arithmetic operators and variables to create **expressions**. The computer evaluates each expression, and the result is a value. To give you an idea of how this works, assume that the value of `num1` is 3 and `num2` is 20, and that both are of data type `int`. With this information in mind, study the examples of expressions and their values in Table 2-3:

Expression	Value	Explanation
`num1 + num2`	23	3 + 20 = 23
`num1 - num2`	−17	3 − 20 = −17
`num2 % num1`	2	20 / 3 = 6 remainder 2
`num1 * num2`	60	3 * 20 = 60
`num2 / num1`	6	20 / 3 = 6 (remainder is truncated)
`-num1`	−3	Value of `num1` is 3, therefore `-num1` is −3

Table 2-3 Expressions and values

Assignment Operators and the Assignment Statement

Another type of operator is an **assignment operator**. You use an assignment operator to assign a value to a variable. A statement that assigns a value to a variable is known as an **assignment statement**. In Java, there are several types of assignment operators. The one you will use most often is the = assignment operator, which simply assigns a value to a variable. Table 2-4 lists and explains some of Java's assignment operators.

Operator Name and Symbol	Example	Comment
Assignment =	count = 5;	Places the value on the right side into the memory location named on the left side.
Initialization =	int count = 5;	Places the value on the right side into the memory location named on the left side when the variable is declared.
Assignment +=	num += 20;	Equivalent to num = num + 20;
Assignment -=	num -= 20;	Equivalent to num = num - 20;
Assignment *=	num *= 20;	Equivalent to num = num * 20;
Assignment /=	num /= 20;	Equivalent to num = num / 20;
Assignment %=	num %= 20;	Equivalent to num = num % 20;

Table 2-4   Java assignment operators

When an assignment statement executes, the computer evaluates the expression on the right side of the assignment operator and then assigns the result to the memory location associated with the variable named on the left side of the assignment operator. An example of an assignment statement is shown in the following code. Notice that the statement ends with a semicolon. In Java, assignment statements always end with a semicolon.

```
answer = num1 * num2;
```

This assignment statement causes the computer to evaluate the expression num1 * num2. After evaluating the expression, the computer stores the results in the memory location associated with answer. If the value stored in the variable named num1 is 3, and the value stored in the variable named num2 is 20, then the value 60 is assigned to the variable named answer.

Here is another example:

```
answer += num1;
```

This statement is equivalent to the following statement:

```
answer = answer + num1;
```

If the value of `answer` is currently 10 and the value of `num1` is 3, then the expression on the right side of the assignment statement `answer + num1;` evaluates to 13, and the computer assigns the value 13 to `answer`.

Precedence and Associativity

Once you start to write code that includes operators, you need to be aware of the order in which a series of operations is performed. In other words, you need to be aware of the **precedence** of operations in your code. Each operator is assigned a certain level of precedence. For example, multiplication has a higher level of precedence than addition. So in the expression `3 * 7 + 2`, the `3 * 7` would be multiplied first; only after the multiplication was completed would the 2 be added.

But what happens when two operators have the same precedence? The rules of **associativity** determine the order in which operations are evaluated in an expression containing two or more operators with the same precedence. For example, in the expression, `3 + 7 - 2`, the addition and subtraction operators have the same precedence. As shown in Table 2-5, the addition and subtraction operators have left-to-right associativity, which causes the expression to be evaluated from left to right (`3 + 7` added first; then 2 is subtracted). Table 2-5 shows the precedence and associativity of the operators discussed in this chapter.

Operator Name	Operator Symbol	Order of Precedence	Associativity
Parentheses	( )	First	Left to right
Unary	− +	Second	Right to left
Multiplication, division, and modulus	* / %	Third	Left to right
Addition and subtraction	+ −	Fourth	Left to right
Assignment	= += −= *= /= %=	Fifth	Right to left

Table 2-5 Order of precedence and associativity

As you can see in Table 2-5, the parentheses operator, ( ), has the highest precedence. You use this operator to change the order in which operations are performed. Note the following example:

```
average = test1 + test2 / 2;
```

The task of this statement is to find the average of two test scores. The way this statement is currently written, the compiler will divide the value in the test2 variable by 2, and then add it to the value in the test1 variable. So, for example, if the value of test1 is 90 and the value of test2 is 88, then the value assigned to average will be 134, which is obviously not the correct average of these two test scores. By using the parentheses operator in this example, you can force the addition to occur before the division. The correct statement looks like this:

```
average = (test1 + test2) / 2;
```

In this example, the value of test1, 90, is added to the value of test2, 88, and then the sum is divided by 2. The value assigned to average, 89, is the correct result.

Exercise 2-4: Understanding Operator Precedence and Associativity

In this exercise, you use what you have learned about operator precedence and associativity in Java. Study the following code and then answer Questions 1–2.

```java
// This program demonstrates the precedence and
// associativity of operators.
public class Operators
{
    public static void main(String args[])
    {
        int value1 = 8;
        int value2 = 2;
        int value3 = 11;
        int answer1, answer2, answer3;
        int answer4, answer5, answer6;

        answer1 = value1 * value2 + value3;
        System.out.println("Answer 1: " + answer1);

        answer2 = value1 * (value2 + value3);
        System.out.println("Answer 2: " + answer2);

        answer3 = value1 + value2 - value3;
        System.out.println("Answer 3: " + answer3);

        answer4 = value1 + (value2 - value3);
        System.out.println("Answer 4: " + answer4);
```

```
        answer5 = value1 + value2 * value3;
        System.out.println("Answer 5: " + answer5);

        answer6 = value3 / value2;
        System.out.println("Answer 6: " + answer6);
        System.exit(0);
    }
}
```

1. What is the value of answer1? answer2? answer3? answer4?
    answer5? and answer6?

    _____

2. Explain how precedence and associativity affect the result.

    _____
    _____
    _____
    _____
    _____

LAB 2.3 Arithmetic and Assignment Operators

In this lab, you complete a partially written Java program
that is provided along with the data files for this book. The
program, which was written for an appliance company, prints the
name of an appliance, its retail price, its wholesale price, the profit
made on the appliance, a sale price, and the profit made when the sale
price is used.

1. Open the file named Appliance.java using Notepad or the
    text editor of your choice.

2. The file includes variable declarations and output statements.
    Read them carefully before you proceed to the next step.

3. Design the logic that will use assignment statements to first
    calculate the profit, then calculate the sale price, and finally
    calculate the profit when the sale price is used. Profit is defined
    as the retail price minus the wholesale price. The sale price is
    20% deducted from the retail price. The sale profit is defined as
    the sale price minus the wholesale price. Perform the appropri-
    ate calculations as part of your assignment statements.

4. Save the source code file in a directory of your choice, and
    then make that directory your working directory.

5. Compile the program.

6. Execute the program. Your output should be as follows:

- Item Name: Dish Washer

- Retail Price: $425.0

- Wholesale Price: $275.0

- Profit: $150.0

- Sale Price: $340.0

- Sale Profit: $65.0

Next, you will see how to put together all you have learned in this chapter to write a Java program that uses sequential statements, comments, and interactive input statements.

Sequential Statements, Comments, and Interactive Input Statements

The term **sequential statements** (or **sequence**) refers to a series of statements that must be performed in sequential order, one after another. You use a sequence in programs when you want to perform actions one after the other. A sequence can contain any number of actions, but those actions must be in the proper order, and no action in the sequence can be skipped. Note that a sequence can contain comments, which are not considered part of the sequence itself.

You are responsible for including well-written, meaningful comments in all of the programs that you write. In fact, some people think that commenting your source code is as important as the source code itself.

Comments serve as documentation, explaining the code to the programmer and any other people who might read it. In Chapter 2 of your book, *Programming Logic and Design, Sixth Edition*, you learned about program comments, which are statements that do not execute. You use comments in Java programs to explain your logic to people who read your source code. The Java compiler ignores comments.

You can choose from two commenting styles in Java. In the first, you type two forward slash characters (//) at the beginning of each line that you want the compiler to ignore. This style is useful when you only want to mark a single line as a comment. In the second style, you enclose a block of lines with the characters /* and */. This style is useful when you want to mark several lines as a comment. You may place comments anywhere in a Java program.

The Java program in the following example shows both styles of comments included in the Temperature program. The first six lines of the program make up a multiline, block comment that explains some basic information about the program. Additionally, several single-line comments are included throughout to describe various parts of the program.

A sequence often includes **interactive input statements**, which are statements that ask, or prompt, the user to input data. The Java program in the following example uses sequential statements and interactive input statements to convert a Fahrenheit temperature to its Celsius equivalent:

```
/* Temperature.java - This program converts a Fahrenheit
   temperature to Celsius.
   Input: Interactive
   Output: Fahrenheit temperature followed by Celsius
   temperature
*/
import javax.swing.JOptionPane; // Import JOptionPane class
public class Temperature
{
    public static void main(String args[])
    {
        String fahrenheitString;
        double fahrenheit;
        double celsius;

        // Get interactive user input
        fahrenheitString = JOptionPane.showInputDialog(
                        "Enter Fahrenheit temperature: ");
        // Convert String to double
        fahrenheit = Double.parseDouble(fahrenheitString);
        // Calculate Celsius equivalent
        celsius = (fahrenheit - 32.0) * (5.0/9.0);
        // Output
        System.out.println("Fahrenheit temperature:" +
                        fahrenheit);
        System.out.println("Celsius temperature:" + celsius);
        // End program
        System.exit(0);
    }
}
```

This program is made up of sequential statements that execute one after the other. As noted above, it also includes comments explaining the code. The comments are those lines enclosed within the /* and */ characters, as well as those lines that begin with //. After the variable fahrenheitString is declared as a String, and fahrenheit and celsius are declared (using the double data type), the following assignment statement executes:

```
fahrenheitString = JOptionPane.showInputDialog(
                "Enter Fahrenheit temperature: ");
```

The showInputDialog method used (on the right side of the assignment statement) belongs to the JOptionPane class and is used when you want the program's user to interactively input data needed by your program. This method may be used in this program because the JOptionPane class was imported into this program using the following statement: import javax.swing.JOptionPane;. When you **import** a class, you give your program access to the methods that are part of the imported class. When you use the showInputDialog() method, you specify within the parentheses the words you want to appear in the dialog box on the user's screen. In this example, the phrase "Enter Fahrenheit temperature:" will appear in the dialog box on the user's screen. The same dialog box also displays a text box where the user can type his or her input, as shown in Figure 2-2.

Figure 2-2 An input dialog box

In this program, you want the user to input a Fahrenheit temperature value so that the program can convert it to Celsius. You would think, then, that this would be a simple matter of taking the value entered by the user, assigning it to a variable, and then performing the necessary conversion calculation. However, Java considers any input entered into an input dialog box to be a String. In this case, the Fahrenheit value input by the user is assigned to the String variable named fahrenheitString. The problem is that we can't perform calculations on Strings; we can only perform calculations on numeric variables. So, before the program can proceed with the calculation required to convert a Fahrenheit value to a Celsius value, we need to transfer the value entered by the user to a variable with a numeric data type.

That task is performed by the following assignment statement, which is the second statement to execute:

```
fahrenheit = Double.parseDouble(fahrenheitString);
```

The parseDouble() method is used on the right side of this assignment statement. This method belongs to the Double class and is used to convert the Fahrenheit value, which the compiler automatically considered a String, to the double data type. Once the String is converted to double, it is assigned to the variable fahrenheit (which, at the beginning of the program, was declared as a double).

The third statement to execute is another assignment statement, as follows:

```
celsius = (fahrenheit - 32.0) * (5.0 / 9.0);
```

The formula that converts Fahrenheit temperatures to Celsius is used on the right side of this assignment statement. Notice the use of parentheses in the expression to control precedence. The expression is evaluated, and the resulting value is assigned to the variable named `celsius`.

Notice that the division uses the values 5.0 and 9.0. This is an example of floating-point division, which results in a value that includes a fraction. If the values 5 and 9 were used, integer division would be performed, and the fractional portion would be truncated.

The next two statements to execute in sequence are both output statements, as follows:

```
System.out.println("Fahrenheit temperature:" +
                    fahrenheit);
System.out.println("Celsius temperature:" + celsius);
```

The statement `System.out.println()` is used to output whatever is within the parentheses. The first output statement displays the words "Fahrenheit temperature:" followed by the value stored in the variable `fahrenheit`. The second output statement displays the words "Celsius temperature:" followed by the value stored in the variable `celsius`. To use the `println()` method correctly, you include only one argument within the parentheses. Arguments are discussed in more detail in Chapter 9. The concatenation operator is used in both output statements to combine two items into one (a string constant, which is one or more characters within double quotes, and a `double`). The + symbol, when used in this context, is the **concatenation** operator, not the addition operator. It is used to combine two values next to each other to create a single string.

In *Programming Logic and Design*, *Sixth Edition*, the comma (`,`) is used as the concatenation operator.

The last statement in this program is `System.exit(0);`. This statement is used to end or terminate a Java program.

This program is saved in a file named `Temperature.java` and is included in the student files for this chapter. You can see the output produced by the Temperature program in Figure 2-3.

You will learn how to control the number of places after the decimal point when you output floating-point values in Chapter 9 of this book.

Figure 2-3 Output from `Temperature.java` program

Now that you have seen a complete Java program that uses sequential statements and interactive input statements, it is time for you to begin writing your own programs.

29

Exercise 2-5: Understanding Sequential Statements

In this exercise, you use what you have learned about sequential statements to read a scenario and then answer Questions 1–4.

Suppose you have written a Java program that calculates the amount of paint you need to cover the walls in your family room. Two walls are 10 feet high and 18.5 feet wide. The other two walls are 10 feet high and 20.5 feet wide. The salesperson at the home improvement store told you to buy 1 gallon of paint for every 150 square feet of wall you need to paint. Suppose you wrote the following code, but your program is not compiling. This program is saved in a file named Paint.java and is included in the student files for this chapter. Take a few minutes to study this code and then answer Questions 1–4.

```java
// Calculates the number of gallons of paint needed.
public class Paint
{
    public static void main(String args[])
    {
        double height1 = 10;
        double height2 = 10;
        int width1 = 18.5;
        double width2 = 20.5;
        double squareFeet;
        int numGallons;
        numGallons = squareFeet / 150;
        squareFeet = (width1 * height1 + width2 * height2) * 2;
        System.out.println("Number of Gallons: " + numGallons);
        System.exit(0);
    }
}
```

1. The first error you receive from the javac compiler is as follows:

    ```
    Paint.java:8: possible loss of precision
    found :double
    required: int
      int width1 = 18.5;
    ```

    What do you have to do to fix this problem? _____

2. The second error you receive from the javac compiler is this:

    ```
    Paint.java:12: possible loss of precision
    found :double
    required: int
      numGallons = squareFeet / 150;
    ```

    What must you do to fix this problem? _____

3. Even if you fix the problems identified in Question 1 and Question 2, you still have a problem with this program. It has to do with the order in which your statements are written. Identify the problem, and then determine what you need to do to fix the problem. On the following lines, describe how to fix the problem.

_____

_____

_____

4. You have two variables declared in this program to represent the height of your walls, height1 and height2. Do you need both of these variables? If not, how would you change the program? Be sure to identify all of the changes you would make.

_____

_____

_____

_____

_____

LAB 2.4 Using Sequential Statements in a Java Program

In this lab, you complete a Java program provided with the data files for this book. The program calculates the amount of tax withheld from an employee's weekly salary, the tax deduction to which the employee is entitled for each dependent, and the employee's take-home pay. The program output includes state tax withheld, federal tax withheld, dependent tax deductions, salary, and take-home pay.

1. Open the source code file named Payroll.java using Notepad or the text editor of your choice.

2. Variables have been declared and initialized for you as needed, and the output statements have been written. Read the code carefully before you proceed to the next step.

3. Write the Java code needed to perform the following:

   • Calculate state withholding tax at 3.0%, and calculate federal withholding tax at 30.0%.

   • Calculate dependent deductions at 5.0% of the employee's salary for each dependent.

- Calculate total withholding.
- Calculate take-home pay as salary minus total withholding plus deductions.

4. Save this source code file in a directory of your choice, and then make that directory your working directory.

5. Compile the program.

6. Execute the program. You should get the following output:

   - State Tax: $28.5

   - Federal Tax: $285.0

   - Dependents: $142.5

   - Salary: $950.0

   - Take-Home Pay: $779.0

7. In this program, the variables named `salary` and `numDependents` are initialized with the values 950.0 and 3. To make this program more flexible, modify it to accept interactive input for `salary` and `numDependents`. Name the modified version `Payroll2.java`.

CHAPTER 3

Writing Structured Java Programs

After studying this chapter, you will be able to:

◎ Use structured flow charts and pseudocode to write structured Java programs

◎ Write simple modular programs in Java

In this chapter, you begin to learn how to write structured Java programs. As you will see, creating a flowchart and writing pseudocode before you actually write the program ensures that you fully understand the program's intended design. We begin by looking at a structured flowchart and pseudocode from your text, *Programming Logic and Design, Sixth Edition*. You should do the exercises and labs in this chapter only after you have finished Chapters 2 and 3 of that book.

Using Flowcharts and Pseudocode to Write a Java Program

In the first three chapters of *Programming Logic and Design, Sixth Edition*, you studied flowcharts and pseudocode for the Number-Doubling program. Figure 3-1 shows the functional, structured flowchart and pseudocode for this program.

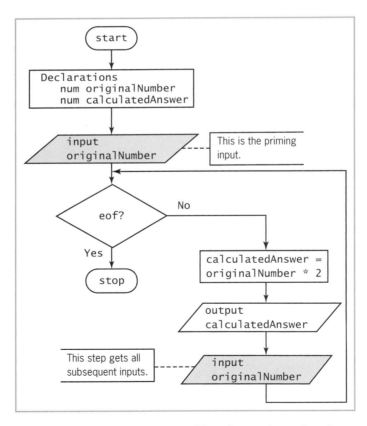

Figure 3-1　Functional, structured flowchart and pseudocode for the Number-Doubling program

By studying the flowchart and pseudocode, you can see that this program makes use of the sequence and loop structures introduced to you in *Programming Logic and Design, Sixth Edition*. The remainder of this section walks you through the Java code for this program. The explanations assume that you are simply reading along, but if you want, you can type the code as it is presented. The goal of this section is to help you get a feel for how flowcharts and pseudocode can serve as a guide as you write Java programs. You must learn more about Java before you can expect to write this program by yourself.

In Figure 3-1, the first line of the pseudocode is the word `start`. How do we translate this pseudocode command into the Java code that will start the Number-Doubling program? In Chapter 1 of this book, you learned that, to start a Java program, you first create a class. So to start the Number-Doubling program, we will first create a class named `NumberDouble`. We should also include one method in the class named `main()` because it is always the first method that executes in a Java program. Thus, the code that follows starts the Number-Doubling program by creating a class named `NumberDouble` and including the `main()` method:

```
public class NumberDouble
{
    public static void main(String args[])
    {

    }
}
```

 Notice in this code that each opening curly brace is matched by a closing curly brace.

Next, you see that two variables, `originalNumber` and `calculatedAnswer`, are declared as data type `num`. The Java code that follows adds the variable declarations with the declarations shown in bold.

```
public class NumberDouble
{
    public static void main(String args[])
    {
        int originalNumber;
        int calculatedAnswer;
    }
}
```

The next line of the pseudocode instructs you to input the `originalNumber`. In other words, you need to write the input statement that primes the loop. You learned about priming read statements in Chapter 3 of *Programming Logic and Design, Sixth Edition*. In Chapter 2 of this book, you learned how to use interactive input statements in programs to allow the user to input data. You also learned to prompt the user by explaining what the program expects to receive as input. The following example includes the code that

 If you are typing the code as it is presented here, save the program in a file that has the same name as the class, for example, `NumberDouble.java`. The complete program is also saved in a file named `NumberDouble.java` and is included in the student files for this chapter.

implements the priming read by displaying a dialog box where users can input the number they want doubled. The next statement converts the input `String` to an `int`.

Note that the code in boldface has been added to the `NumberDouble` class. The `String` variable named `originalNumberString` is added to hold the input entered into the input dialog box. If you were writing this code yourself, you would start by writing the code for the `NumberDouble` class, and then edit it to add the boldface code show here:

```
import javax.swing.JOptionPane;
public class NumberDouble
{
    public static void main(String args[])
    {
        int originalNumber;
        String originalNumberString;
        int calculatedAnswer;
        originalNumberString = JOptionPane.showInputDialog(
                            "Enter number to double: ");
        originalNumber = Integer.parseInt(originalNumberString);
    }
}
```

Next, the pseudocode instructs you to begin a `while` loop with `eof` (end of file) used as the condition to exit the loop.

Since we are using interactive input in this program, it requires no `eof` marker. Instead we will use the number 0 (zero) to indicate the end of input. We'll use 0 because 0 doubled will always be 0. The use of 0 to indicate the end of input also requires us to change the prompt to tell the user how to end the program. Review the following code. Again, the newly added code is formatted in bold.

```
import javax.swing.JOptionPane;
public class NumberDouble
{
    public static void main(String args[])
    {
        int originalNumber;
        String originalNumberString;
        int calculatedAnswer;
        originalNumberString = JOptionPane.showInputDialog(
                    "Enter number to double or 0 to end: ");
        originalNumber = Integer.parseInt(
                            originalNumberString);
        while(originalNumber != 0)
        {
        }
    }
}
```

You have not learned enough about `while` loops to write this code yourself, but you can observe how it is done in this example. You will learn more about loops in Chapter 5 of this book.

A beginning curly brace ({) and an ending curly brace (}) are used in Java to mark the beginning and end of code that executes as part of a loop.

According to the pseudocode, the body of the loop is made up of three sequential statements. The first statement calculates the originalNumber multiplied by 2; the second statement prints the calculatedAnswer; and the third statement retrieves the next originalNumber from the user. In Java, we actually need to add a fourth statement between the curly braces that mark the body of the while loop. This fourth statement converts the input String to an int.

In the following example, the code that makes up the body of the loop is in bold.

```
import javax.swing.JOptionPane;
public class NumberDouble
{
    public static void main(String args[])
    {
        int originalNumber;
        String originalNumberString;
        int calculatedAnswer;
        originalNumberString = JOptionPane.showInputDialog(
                    "Enter number to double or 0 to end: ");
        originalNumber = Integer.parseInt(originalNumberString);
        while(originalNumber != 0)
        {
            calculatedAnswer = originalNumber * 2;
            System.out.println(originalNumber + " doubled is "
                        + calculatedAnswer);
            originalNumberString = JOptionPane.showInputDialog(
                    "Enter number to double or 0 to end: ");
            originalNumber = Integer.parseInt(
                        originalNumberString);
        }
    }
}
```

The last line of the pseudocode instructs you to end the program. In Java, the closing curly brace (}) for the main() method signifies the end of the program. Note that the preceding code includes three closing curly braces. The last one is the one that ends the NumberDouble class, and the second-to-last one ends the main() method.

At this point, the program is ready to be compiled. Assuming there are no syntax errors, it should execute as planned. Figure 3-2 displays the input and output of the program.

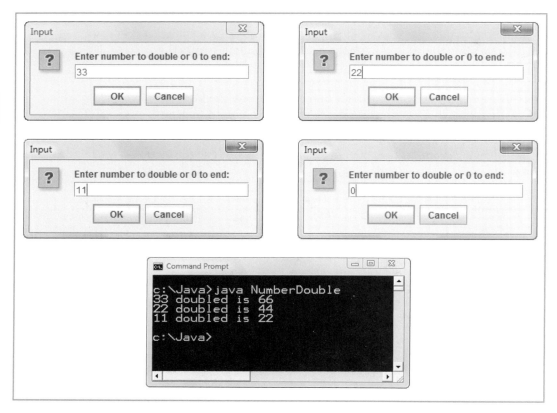

Figure 3-2   Number Double program input and output

Although you have not learned everything you need to know to write this program yourself, you can see from this example that writing the program in Java is easier if you start with a well-designed, functional, structured flowchart or pseudocode.

LAB 3.1   Using Flowcharts and Pseudocode to Write a Java Program

In this lab, you use the pseudocode in Figure 3-3 to add code to a partially created Java program. When completed, college admissions officers should be able to use the Java program to determine whether to accept or reject a student, based on his or her class rank.

```
start
   input testScore, classRank
   if testScore >= 90 then
      if classRank >= 25 then
         output "Accept"
      else
         output "Reject"
      endif
   else
      if testScore >= 80 then
         if classRank >= 50 then
            output "Accept"
         else
            output "Reject"
         endif
      else
         if testScore >= 70 then
            if classRank >= 75 then
               output "Accept"
            else
               output "Reject"
            endif
         else
            output "Reject"
         endif
      endif
   endif
stop
```

Figure 3-3   Pseudocode for the College Admission program

1. Study the pseudocode in Figure 3-3.

2. Open the source code file named `CollegeAdmission.java` using Notepad or the text editor of your choice.

3. Declare two String variables named `testScoreString` and `classRankString`.

4. Declare two integer variables named `testScore` and `classRank`.

5. Write the interactive input statements to retrieve a student's test score and class rank from the user of the program.

6. Write the statements to convert the `String` representation of a student's test score and class rank to the integer data type.

7. The rest of the program is written for you. Save this source code file in a directory of your choice, and then make that directory your working directory.

8. Compile the source code file CollegeAdmission.java.

9. Execute the program by entering 30 for the test score and 95 for the class rank. Record the output of this program.

---

10. Execute the program by entering 95 for the test score and 30 for the class rank. Record the output of this program.

Writing a Modular Program in Java

In Chapter 2 of your book, *Programming Logic and Design, Sixth Edition*, you learned about local and global variables and named constants. To review briefly, you declare **local variables** and local constants within the module—or, in Java terminology, the method—that uses them. Further, you can only use a local variable or a local constant within the method in which it is declared. (Note that, in this book, we use the term "method" instead of "module," as this is the term used in the Java programming language.) **Global variables** and global constants are known to an entire program; they are declared at the program level and are visible to and usable in all the methods called by the program. Java does not allow for the use of global variables or global constants, so the program below uses local variables (as well as local constants).

Also, recall from Chapter 2 that most programs consist of a main method, which contains the mainline logic. The mainline logic of most procedural programs follows this general structure:

1. Declarations of variables and constants

2. **Housekeeping tasks**, such as displaying instructions to users, displaying report headings, opening files the program requires, and inputting the first data item

3. **Detail loop tasks** that do the main work of the program, such as processing many records and performing calculations

4. **End-of-job tasks**, such as displaying totals and closing any open files

In Chapter 2 of *Programming Logic and Design, Sixth Edition*, you studied a flowchart and pseudocode for a modular program that prints a payroll report for a small company, using global variables and constants. This flowchart and pseudocode is shown in Figure 3-4.

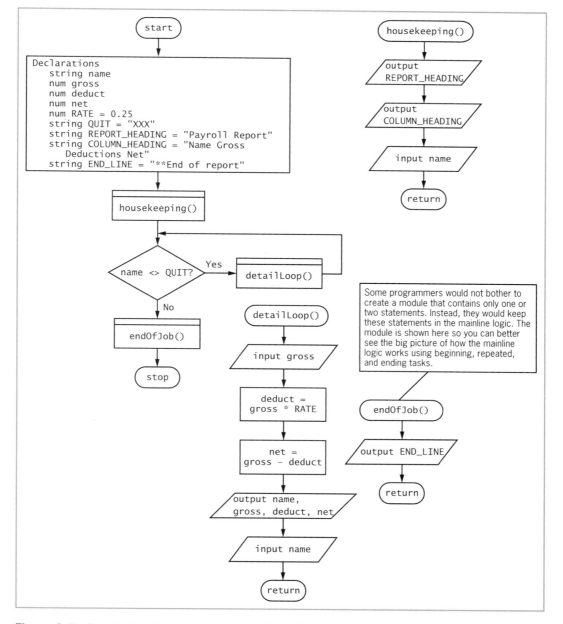

Figure 3-4 Flowchart and pseudocode for the Payroll Report program *(continues)*

(continued)

```
start
   Declarations
      string name
      num gross
      num deduct
      num net
      num RATE = 0.25
      string QUIT = "XXX"
      string REPORT_HEADING = "Payroll Report"
      string COLUMN_HEADING = "Name  Gross  Deductions  Net"
      string END_LINE = "**End of report"
   housekeeping()
   while not name = QUIT
      detailLoop()
   endwhile
   endOfJob()
stop

housekeeping()
   output REPORT_HEADING
   output COLUMN_HEADING
   input name
return

detailLoop()
   input gross
   deduct = gross * RATE
   net = gross - deduct
   output name, gross, deduct, net
   input name
return

endOfJob()
   output END_LINE
return
```

Figure 3-4 Flowchart and pseudocode for the Payroll Report program

In this section, we walk through the process of creating a Java program that implements the logic illustrated in Figure 3-4. According to the flowchart, the program begins with the execution of the mainline method. The mainline method in the flowchart declares four global variables (name, gross, deduct, and net) and five global constants (RATE, QUIT, REPORT_HEADING, COLUMN_HEADING, and END_LINE). The Java code that follows shows the creation of the PayrollReport class, the main() method, and variable and constant declarations.

```
import javax.swing.JOptionPane;
public class PayrollReport
{
    public static void main(String args[])
    {
        String name;
        String grossString;
        double gross, deduct, net;
        final double RATE = 0.25;
        final String QUIT = "XXX";
        final String REPORT_HEADING = "Payroll Report";
        final String END_LINE = "**End of report";
    }
}
```

If you are typing the code as it is presented here, save the program in a file that has the same name as the class, for example, PayrollReport.java. The complete program is also saved in a file named PayrollReport.java and is included in the student files for this chapter.

43

Notice that one of the declarations shown in the flowchart, `string COLUMN_HEADING = "Name Gross Deductions Net,"` is not included in the Java code. Since you have not yet learned about the Java statements needed to line up values in report format, the Java program shown above prints information on separate lines rather than in the column format used in the flowchart. Also, notice that the Java code includes one additional variable, `grossString`, which is used to hold the user-entered value for an employee's gross pay. Later in the program, the `String` variable, `grossString`, is converted to a `double` so that it may be used in calculations.

It is important for you to understand that the variables and constants declared in the flowchart are global variables that may be used in all methods that are part of the program. However, as mentioned earlier, Java does not allow for the use of global variables. The variables and constants declared in the Java version are local, which means they may only be used in the `main()` method.

After the declarations, the pseudocode makes a call to the `housekeeping()` module that prints the REPORT_HEADING and COLUMN_HEADING constants and retrieves the first employee's name entered by the user of the program. The code that follows shows how these tasks are translated to Java statements. The added code is shown in bold.

```
import javax.swing.JOptionPane;
public class PayrollReport
{
    public static void main(String args[])
    {
        String name;
        String grossString;
        double gross, deduct, net;
        final double RATE = 0.25;
        final String QUIT = "XXX";
        final String REPORT_HEADING = "Payroll Report";
        final String END_LINE = "**End of report";
        // This is the work done in the housekeeping() method
        System.out.println(REPORT_HEADING);
        name = JOptionPane.showInputDialog(
                "Enter employee's name: ");
    }
}
```

Since Java does not allow for global variables, all of the variables declared for this program are local variables that are available only in the main() method. If we were to create an additional method for the housekeeping tasks, that method would not have access to the name variable to store an employee's name. So, for now, the Java programs that you write will have only one method (module), the main() method. Additional modules, such as the housekeeping() module, will be simulated through the use of comments. As shown in the preceding code, the statements that would execute as part of a housekeeping() method have been grouped together in the Java program and preceded by a comment. You will learn how to create additional methods and pass data to methods in Chapter 9 of this book.

In the flowchart, the next statement to execute after the housekeeping() module finishes its work is a while loop in the main module that continues to execute until the user enters "XXX" when prompted for an employee's name. Within the loop, the detailLoop() module is called. The work done in the detailLoop() consists of retrieving an employee's gross pay, calculating deductions; calculating net pay; printing the employee's name, gross pay, deductions, and net pay on the user's screen; and retrieving the name of the next employee. The following code shows the Java statements that have been added to the Payroll Report program to implement this logic. The added statements are shown in bold.

```
import javax.swing.JOptionPane;
public class PayrollReport
{
    public static void main(String args[])
    {
        String name;
        String grossString;
        double gross, deduct, net;
        final double RATE = 0.25;
        final String QUIT = "XXX";
        final String REPORT_HEADING = "Payroll Report";
        final String END_LINE = "**End of report";
        // This is the work done in the housekeeping() method
        System.out.println(REPORT_HEADING);
        name = JOptionPane.showInputDialog(
                        "Enter employee's name: ");
        while(name.compareTo(QUIT) != 0)
        {
            // This is the work done in the detailLoop() method
            grossString = JOptionPane.showInputDialog(
                        "Enter employee's gross pay: ");
            gross = Double.parseDouble(grossString);
            deduct = gross * RATE;
            net = gross - deduct;
            System.out.println("Name: " + name);
            System.out.println("Gross Pay: " + gross);
            System.out.println("Deductions: " + deduct);
            System.out.println("Net Pay: " + net);
            name = JOptionPane.showInputDialog(
                    "Enter employee's name: ");
        }
    }
}
```

The while loop in the Java program uses the compareTo() method to compare the name entered by the user with the value of the constant named QUIT. As long as the name is not equal to "XXX" (the value of QUIT), the loop executes. The statements that make up the simulated detailLoop() method include: retrieving the employee's gross pay; converting the grossString value to a Double using the parseDouble() method; calculating deductions and net pay; printing the employee's name, gross pay, deductions, and net pay; and retrieving the name of the next employee to process.

In the flowchart, when a user enters "XXX" for the employee's name, the program exits the while loop and then calls the endOfJob() module. The endOfJob() module is responsible for printing the value of the END_LINE constant. When the endOfJob() module finishes, control returns to the mainline module, and the program stops. The completed Java program is shown next with the additional statement shown in bold.

You learn more about the compareTo() method in Chapter 4.

You learned about the method named parseDouble() in Chapter 2.

```java
import javax.swing.JOptionPane;
public class PayrollReport
{
   public static void main(String args[])
   {
      String name;
      String grossString;
      double gross, deduct, net;
      final double RATE = 0.25;
      final String QUIT = "XXX";
      final String REPORT_HEADING = "Payroll Report";
      final String END_LINE = "**End of report";
      // This is the work done in the housekeeping() method
      System.out.println(REPORT_HEADING);
      name = JOptionPane.showInputDialog(
            "Enter employee's name: ");
      while(name.compareTo(QUIT) != 0)
      {
        // This is the work done in the detailLoop() method
        grossString = JOptionPane.showInputDialog(
                    "Enter employee's gross pay: ");
        gross = Double.parseDouble(grossString);
        deduct = gross * RATE;
        net = gross - deduct;
        System.out.println("Name: " + name);
        System.out.println("Gross Pay: " + gross);
        System.out.println("Deductions: " + deduct);
        System.out.println("Net Pay: " + net);
        name = JOptionPane.showInputDialog(
              "Enter employee's name: ");
      }
      // This is the work done in the endOfJob() method
      System.out.println(END_LINE);
   }
}
```

This program is now complete. Figure 3-5 shows the program's output in response to the input "William" (for the name), and 1200 (for the gross).

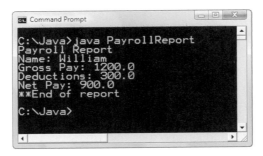

Figure 3-5 Output of the Payroll Report program when the input is "William" and 1200

LAB 3.2 Writing a Modular Program in Java

In this lab, you add the input and output statements to a partially completed Java program. When completed, the user should be able to enter a year and then click the "OK" button, enter a month and then click the "OK" button, and enter a day and then click the "OK" button to determine if the date is valid. Valid years are those that are greater than 0, valid months include the values 1 through 12, and valid days include the values 1 through 31.

1. Open the source code file named BadDate.java using Notepad or the text editor of your choice.

2. Notice that variables have been declared for you.

3. Write the simulated housekeeping() method that contains input statements to retrieve a year, a month, and a day from the user.

4. Add statements to the simulated housekeeping() method that convert the String representation of the year, month, and day to ints.

5. Include the output statements in the simulated endOfJob() method. The format of the output is as follows:

   month/day/year is a valid date.
   or
   month/day/year is an invalid date.

6. Save this source code file in a directory of your choice, and then make that directory your working directory.

7. Compile the source code file BadDate.java.

8. Execute the program entering the following date: month = 7, day = 24, year = 2011. Record the output of this program.

   _____

9. Execute the program entering the following date: month = 9, day = 21, year = 2002. Record the output of this program.

   _____

Writing Programs that Make Decisions

After studying this chapter, you will be able to:

◎ Use relational and logical Boolean operators to make decisions in a program

◎ Compare `String` objects

◎ Write decision statements in Java, including an `if` statement, an `if-else` statement, nested `if` statements, and the `switch` statement

◎ Use decision statements to make multiple comparisons by using AND logic and OR logic

You should complete the exercises and labs in this chapter only after you have finished Chapter 4 of your book, *Programming Logic and Design, Sixth Edition*. In this chapter, you practice using Java's relational and logical operators as well as `String` methods to write Boolean expressions. You also learn the Java syntax for decision statements, including the `if` statement, the `if-else` statement, nested `if` statements, and `switch` statements. Finally, you learn to write Java statements that make multiple comparisons.

Boolean Operators

You use Boolean operators in expressions when you want to compare values. When you use a **Boolean operator** in an expression, the evaluation of that expression results in a value that is `true` or `false`. In Java, you can subdivide the Boolean operators into two groups: relational operators and logical operators. We begin the discussion with the relational operators.

Relational Operators

In the context of programming, the term **relational** refers to the connections, or relationships, that values can have with one another. For example, one value might be greater than another, less than another, or equal to the other value. The terms "greater than," "less than," and "equal to" all refer to a relationship between two values. As with all Boolean operators, a relational operator allows you to ask a question that results in a `true` or `false` answer. Depending on the answer, your program will execute different statements that perform different actions.

Table 4-1 lists the relational operators used in Java.

Operator	Meaning
<	Less than
<=	Less than or equal to
>	Greater than
>=	Greater than or equal to
==	Equal to (two equal signs with no space between them)
!=	Not equal to

Table 4-1   Relational operators

To see how to use relational operators, suppose you declare two variables: an `int` named `number1` that you initialize with the value 10 and another `int` variable named `number2` that you initialize with the value 15. The following code shows the declaration statements for these variables:

```
int number1 = 10;
int number2 = 15;
```

The following code samples illustrate how relational operators are used in expressions:

- `number1 < number2` evaluates to `true` because 10 is less than 15.

- `number1 <= number2` evaluates to `true` because 10 is less than or equal to 15.

- `number1 > number2` evaluates to `false` because 10 is not greater than 15.

- `number1 >= number2` evaluates to `false` because 10 is not greater than or equal to 15.

- `number1 == number2` evaluates to `false` because 10 is not equal to 15.

- `number1 != number2` evaluates to `true` because 10 is not equal to 15.

Logical Operators

You can use another type of Boolean operator, **logical operators**, when you need to ask more than one question but you want to receive only one answer. For example, in a program, you may want to ask if a number is between the values 1 and 10. This actually involves two questions. You need to ask if the number is greater than 1 AND if the number is less than 10. Here, you are asking two questions, but you want only one answer—either "yes" (`true`) or "no" (`false`).

Logical operators are useful in decision statements because, like relational expressions, they evaluate to `true` or `false`, thereby permitting decision-making in your programs.

Table 4-2 lists the logical operators used in Java.

Operator	Name	Description
&&	AND	All expressions must evaluate to `true` for the entire expression to be `true`; this operator is written as two & symbols with no space between them.
||	OR	Only one expression must evaluate to `true` for the entire expression to be `true`; this operator is written as two | symbols with no space between them.
!	NOT	This operator reverses the value of the expression; if the expression evaluates to `false`, then reverse it so that the expression evaluates to `true`.

Table 4-2　Logical operators

To see how to use the logical operators, suppose you declare two
variables: an `int` named `number1` that you initialize with the value 10;
and another `int` variable named `number2` that you initialize with the
value 15. The declaration statements for these variables are shown in
the following code:

```
int number1 = 10;
int number2 = 15;
```

The following code samples illustrate how you can use the logical
operators along with the relational operators in expressions:

- `(number1 > number2) || (number1 == 10)` evaluates to `true`
  because the first expression evaluates to `false`, 10 is not greater
  than 15, and the second expression evaluates to `true`, 10 is equal
  to 10. Only one expression needs to be `true` using OR logic for the
  entire expression to be `true`.

- `(number1 > number2) && (number1 == 10)` evaluates to `false`
  because the first expression is `false`, 10 is not greater than 15, and
  the second expression is `true`, 10 is equal to 10. Using AND logic,
  both expressions must be `true` for the entire expression to be `true`.

- `(number1 != number2) && (number1 == 10)` evaluates to `true`
  because both expressions are `true`; that is, 10 is not equal to 15,
  and 10 is equal to 10. Using AND logic, if both expressions are
  `true`, then the entire expression is `true`.

- `!(number1 == number2)` evaluates to `true` because the expression
  evaluates to `false`, 10 is not equal to 15. The `!` operator then
  reverses `false`, which results in a `true` value.

Relational and Logical Operator Precedence and Associativity

Like the arithmetic operators discussed in Chapter 2, the relational
and logical operators are evaluated according to specific rules of
associativity and precedence. Table 4-3 shows the precedence and
associativity of the operators discussed thus far in this book.

Operator Name	Symbol	Order of Precedence	Associativity
Parentheses	( )	First	Left to right
Unary	- + !	Second	Right to left
Multiplication, division, and modulus	* / %	Third	Left to right
Addition and subtraction	+ -	Fourth	Left to right
Relational	< > <= >=	Fifth	Left to right
Equality	== !=	Sixth	Left to right
AND	&&	Seventh	Left to right
OR	||	Eighth	Left to right
Assignment	= += -= *= /= %=	Ninth	Right to left

Table 4-3   Order of precedence and associativity

As shown in Table 4-3, the AND operator has a higher precedence than the OR operator, meaning expressions that include the AND operator are evaluated first. Also notice that the relational operators have higher precedence than the equality operators, and both the relational and equality operators have higher precedence than the AND and OR operators. All of these operators have left-to-right associativity.

To see how to use the logical operators and the relational operators in expressions, first assume that the variables `number1` and `number2` are declared and initialized as shown in the following code:

```
int number1 = 10;
int number2 = 15;
```

Now, you write the following expression in Java.

```
number1 == 10 || number2 == number1 && number2 == 15
```

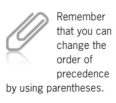

Remember that you can change the order of precedence by using parentheses.

Looking at Table 4-3, you can see that the equality operator (==) has a higher level of precedence than the AND operator (&&), and the AND operator (&&) has a higher level of precedence than the OR operator (||). Also, notice that there are three == operators in the expression; thus, the left-to-right associativity rule applies. Figure 4-1 illustrates the order in which the operators are used.

As you can see in Figure 4-1, it takes five steps, following the rules of precedence and associativity, to determine the value of the expression.

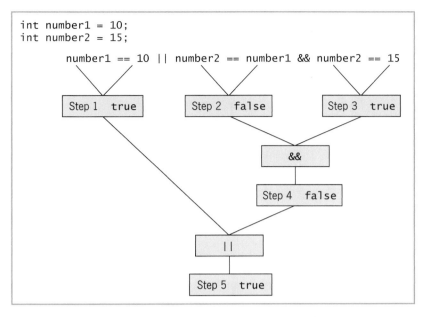

```
int number1 = 10;
int number2 = 15;
```

Figure 4-1   Evaluation of expression using relational and logical operators

Comparing Strings

In Java, you use relational operators when you compare primitive data types such as `ints` and `doubles`. As you have learned, a primitive data type is one that is built into the language. You do not use relational operators to compare `Strings` in Java because this would result in comparing references to the `String` objects, rather than comparing the contents of the `String` objects. (A **reference** is the location in memory where an object is stored.) This is discussed in more detail later in this section.

Two `String` objects are equal when their contents are the same.

When you declare a `String` variable, the declaration instantiates the `String` class and creates a `String` object. The `String` class contains multiple methods you can use when you want to compare `String` objects. One of these methods is the `equals()` method. You use it when you want to test two `String` objects for equality. The `equals()` method returns `true` if the two `String` objects are equal, and `false` if they are not.

The following code shows how to use the `equals()` method to compare two `String` objects and also to compare one `String` object and one string constant.

```
String s1 = "Hello";
String s2 = "World";
```

```
s1.equals(s2);
// Evaluates to false because "Hello" is not the same as
// "World".

s1.equals("Hello");
// Evaluates to true because "Hello" is the same as
// "Hello".
```

In Java, it is important not to use the == operator to compare String objects. Although doing so will not generate an error, it will cause the computer to test to see if two String objects are the same object (i.e., have identical references) instead of whether they have the same contents. The only time one String object would have the same reference value as another is when they are the same object. In other words, this would be like testing to see if String1 is equal to String1, which is a pointless comparison.

Another method used to compare String objects is the compareTo() method. It returns a 0 if two String objects are equal, a value less than 0 if the invoking String object is less than the String object passed to the method, and a value greater than 0 if the invoking String object is greater than the String object passed to the method.

As shown in Figure 4-2, s1 is the invoking String object, and s2 is the String object passed to the method.

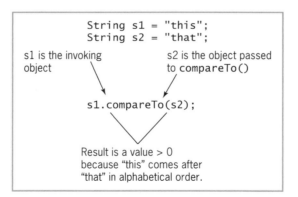

Figure 4-2   Using the compareTo() method

The compareTo() method compares the ASCII values of the individual characters in String objects to determine if one String object is greater than, less than, or equal to another, in terms of alphabetizing the text in the String objects. As shown in Figure 4-2, the String object s1, whose value is "this", is greater than the String object s2, whose value is "that", because "this" comes after "that" in alphabetical order. The result of using the compareTo() method with

String objects s1 and s2 is a value greater than 0 because "this" is greater than "that."

The following code sample shows how to use the compareTo() method with two String objects.

```
String s1 = "whole";
String s2 = "whale";
// The next statement evaluates to a value greater than
// 0 because the contents of s1, "whole", are greater
// than the contents of s2, "whale."
s1.compareTo(s2);
// The next statement evaluates to a value less than 0
// because the contents of s2, "whale", are less than the
// contents of s1, "whole."
s2.compareTo(s1);
```

The following code sample shows how to use the compareTo() method to compare a String object and a string constant.

```
String s1 = "whole";
s1.compareTo("whole"); // Evaluates to 0, because
                       // they are equal.
```

Decision Statements

Every decision in a program is based on whether an expression evaluates to true or false. Programmers use decision statements to change the flow of control in a program. **Flow of control** means the order in which statements are executed. Decision statements are also known as branching statements, because they cause the computer to make a decision, choosing from one or more branches (or paths) in the program.

There are different types of decision statements in Java. We will begin with the if statement.

The if Statement

The if statement is a single-path decision statement. As you learned in *Programming Logic and Design, Sixth Edition*, if statements are also referred to as "single alternative" or "single-sided" statements.

When we use the term **single-path**, we mean that if an expression evaluates to true, your program executes one or more statements, but if the expression evaluates to false, your program will not execute these statements. There is only one defined path—the path taken if the expression evaluates to true. In either case, the statement following the if statement is executed.

The **syntax**, or set of rules, for writing an if statement in Java is as follows:

```
if(expression)
    statementA;
```

Note that when you type the keyword if to begin an if statement, you follow it with an expression placed within parentheses.

When the compiler encounters an if statement, the expression within the parentheses is evaluated. If the expression evaluates to true, then the computer executes *statementA*. If the expression in parentheses evaluates to false, then the computer will not execute *statementA*. Remember that whether the expression evaluates to true and executes *statementA*, or the expression evaluates to false and does not execute *statementA*, the statement following the if statement executes next.

Note that a Java statement, such as an if statement, can be either a simple statement or a block statement. A **block** statement is made up of multiple Java statements. Java defines a block as statements placed within a pair of curly braces. If you want your program to execute more than one statement as part of an if statement, you must enclose the statements in a pair of curly braces or only one statement will execute. The following example illustrates an if statement that uses the relational operator (<) to test if the value of the variable customerAge is less than 65. You will see the first curly brace in the fourth line and the second curly brace in the second-to-last line.

```
int customerAge = 53;
int discount, numUnder;
if(customerAge < 65)
{
    discount = 0;
    numUnder += 1;
}
System.out.println("Discount : " + discount);
```

In the preceding code, the variable named customerAge is initialized to the value 53. Because 53 is less than 65, the expression, customerAge < 65, evaluates to true, and the block statement executes. The block statement is made up of the two assignment statements within the curly braces: discount = 0; and numUnder += 1;. If the expression evaluates to false, the block statement does not execute. In either case, the next statement to execute is the output statement, System.out.println("Discount : " + discount);.

Notice that you do not include a semicolon at the end of the line with the if and the expression to be tested. Including a semicolon at the end of this line would not create a syntax error, but it could create a logic error in your program. A **logic error** causes your program to produce incorrect results. In Java, the semicolon (;) is called the null statement and is considered a legal statement. The **null** statement is a statement that does nothing. Examine the following code:

```
int customerAge = 53;
int discount, numUnder;
if (customerAge < 65 ); // semicolon here is not correct
{
    discount = 0;
    numUnder += 1;
}
```

If you write an `if` statement as shown in the preceding code, your program will test the expression `customerAge < 65`. If it evaluates to `true`, the null statement executes, which means your program does nothing, and then the statement, `discount = 0;` executes because this is the next statement following the `if` statement. This does not cause a logic error in your program, but consider what happens when the expression in the `if` statement evaluates to `false`. If `false`, the null statement does not execute, but the statement `discount = 0;` will execute because it is the next statement after the `if` statement.

The following code uses an `if` statement along with the `equals()` method to test two `String` objects for equality:

```
String dentPlan = "Y";
double grossPay = 500.00
if(dentPlan.equals("Y"))
    grossPay = grossPay - 23.50;
```

In this example, if the value of the `String` object named `dentPlan` and the string constant "Y" are the same value, the expression evaluates to `true`, and the `grossPay` calculation assignment statement executes. If the expression evaluates to `false`, the `grossPay` calculation assignment statement does not execute.

Exercise 4-1: Understanding `if` Statements

In this exercise, you use what you have learned about writing `if` statements. Study the following code and then answer Questions 1–4.

```
// VotingAge.java - This program determines if a
// person is eligible to vote.
public class VotingAge
{
    public static void main(String args[])
    {
        // Work done in the housekeeping() method
        int myAge = 19;
        String ableToVote = "Yes";
        final int VOTING_AGE = 18;
```

```
        // Work done in the detailLoop() method
        if(myAge < VOTING_AGE)
            ableToVote = "No";
        System.out.println("My Age: " + myAge);
        System.out.println("Able To Vote: " + ableToVote);
        // Work done in the endOfJob() method
        System.exit(0);
    }
}
```

1. What is the exact output when this program executes?

    _____

    _____

2. What is the exact output if the value of myAge is changed
    to 15?

    _____

    _____

3. What is the exact output if the expression in the if statement
    is changed to myAge <= VOTING_AGE ?

    _____

    _____

4. What is the exact output if the variable named ableToVote is
    initialized with the value "No" rather than the value "Yes"?

    _____

    _____

LAB 4.1   Using if Statements

In this lab, you complete a prewritten Java program for a
furniture company. The program is supposed to compute
the price of any table a customer orders, based on the
following facts:

- The charge for all tables is a minimum of $120.00.

- If the surface (length * width) is over 700 square inches, add $40.00.

- If the wood is mahogany, add $250.00; for oak, add $150.00. No
  charge is added for pine.

- For extension leaves for the table, there is an additional $60.00
  charge each.

1. Open the file named `Furniture.java` using Notepad or the text editor of your choice.

2. You need to declare variables for the following, and initialize them where specified:

   - A variable for the cost of the table initialized to 0.00.

   - A variable for the length of the table initialized to 50 inches.

   - A variable for the width of the table initialized to 40 inches.

   - A variable for the surface area of the table.

   - A variable for the wood type initialized with the value "oak".

   - A variable for the number of extension leaves initialized with the value 2.

3. Write the rest of the program using assignment statements and `if` statements as appropriate. The output statements are written for you.

4. Compile the program.

5. Execute the program. Your output should be: The charge for this table is $430.0.

Note that you cannot control the number of places that appear after the decimal point until you learn more about Java in Chapter 9 of this book.

The `if-else` Statement

The `if-else` statement is a dual-path or dual-alternative decision statement. That is, your program will take one of two paths as a result of evaluating an expression in an `if-else` statement.

The syntax for writing an `if-else` statement in Java is as follows:

```
if(expression)
    statementA;
else
    statementB;
```

When the compiler encounters an `if-else` statement, the expression in the parentheses is evaluated. If the expression evaluates to `true`, then the computer executes *statementA*. Otherwise, if the expression in parentheses evaluates to `false`, then the computer executes

Do not include a semicolon at the end of the line containing the keyword `if` and the expression to be tested, or on the line with the keyword `else`. While doing so is not a syntax error, it could create a logic error.

59

statementB. Both *statementA* and *statementB* can be simple statements or block statements. Regardless of which path is taken in a program, the statement following the `if-else` statement is the next one to execute.

The following code sample illustrates an `if-else` statement written in Java:

```java
int hoursWorked = 45;
double rate = 15.00;
double grossPay;
String overtime = "Yes";
final int HOURS_IN_WEEK = 40;
final double OVERTIME_RATE = 1.5;
if(hoursWorked > HOURS_IN_WEEK)
{
    overtime = "Yes";
    grossPay = HOURS_IN_WEEK * rate +
        (hoursWorked - HOURS_IN_WEEK) *
        OVERTIME_RATE * rate;
}
else
{
    overtime = "No";
    grossPay = hoursWorked * rate;
}
System.out.println("Overtime: " + overtime);
System.out.println("Gross Pay: $" + grossPay);
```

HOURS_IN _WEEK is a constant that is initialized with the value 40, and OVERTIME_RATE is a constant that is initialized with the value 1.5.

In the preceding code, the value of the variable named `hoursWorked` is tested to see if it is greater than HOURS_IN_WEEK.

You use the greater than relational operator (>) to make the comparison. If the expression, `hoursWorked > HOURS_IN_WEEK`, evaluates to `true`, then the block statement executes. This first block statement contains one statement that assigns the string constant "Yes" to the variable named `overtime`, and another statement that calculates the employee's gross pay, including overtime pay, and assigns the calculated value to the variable named `grossPay`.

If the expression, `hoursWorked > HOURS_IN_WEEK`, evaluates to `false`, then a different path is followed, and the second block statement following the keyword `else` executes. This block statement contains one statement that assigns the string constant "No" to the variable named `overtime` and another statement that calculates the employee's gross pay with no overtime and assigns the calculated value to the variable named `grossPay`.

Regardless of which path is taken, the next statement to execute is the output statement, `System.out.println("Overtime: " + overtime);` immediately followed by the output statement `System.out.println("Gross Pay: $" + grossPay);`.

Exercise 4-2: Understanding `if-else` Statements

In this exercise, you use what you have learned about writing `if-else` statements. This program was written to calculate customer charges for a telephone company. The telephone company charges 20 cents per minute for calls outside of the customer's area code that last over 15 minutes. All other calls are 25 cents per minute. Study the following code and then answer Questions 1–4.

```java
// Telephone.java - This program determines telephone
// call charges.
public class Telephone
{
    public static void main(String args[])
    {
        // This is the work done in the housekeeping() method
        int custAC, custNumber;
        int calledAC, calledNumber;
        int callMinutes;
        double callCharge;
        final int MAX_MINS = 15;
        final double CHARGE_1 = 0.20;
        final double CHARGE_2 = 0.25;
        // This is the work done in the detailLoop() method
        custAC = 630;
        custNumber = 5551234;
        calledAC = 219;
        calledNumber = 5557890;
        callMinutes = 45;
        if(calledAC != custAC && callMinutes > MAX_MINS)
            callCharge = callMinutes * CHARGE_1;
        else
            callCharge = callMinutes * CHARGE_2;
        // This is the work done in the endOfJob() method
        System.out.println("Customer Number: " + custAC +
            "-" + custNumber);
        System.out.println("Called Number: " + calledAC +
            "-" + calledNumber);
        System.out.println("The charge for this call is $"
            + callCharge);
        System.exit(0);
    }
}
```

1. What is the exact output when this program executes?

   _____

   _____

2. What is the exact output if the value of callMinutes is changed to 20?

   _____

   _____

3. What is the exact output if the expression in the if statement is changed to callMinutes >= MAX_MINS?

   _____

   _____

4. What is the exact output if the variable named custAC is assigned the value 219 rather than the value 630?

   _____

   _____

LAB 4.2   Using if-else Statements

In this lab, you will complete a prewritten Java program that computes the largest and smallest of three integer values. The three values are 125, 300, and −10.

1. Open the file named LargeSmall.java using Notepad or the text editor of your choice.

2. Two variables named largest and smallest are declared for you. Use these variables to store the largest and smallest of the three integer values. You must decide what other variables you will need and initialize them if appropriate.

3. Write the rest of the program using assignment statements, if statements, or if-else statements as appropriate. There are comments in the code that tell you where you should write your statements. The output statement is written for you.

4. Compile the program.

5. Execute the program. Your output should be:

    The largest value is 300
    The smallest value is −10

Nested if Statements

You can nest if statements to create a multipath decision statement. When you nest if statements, you include an if statement within another if statement. This is helpful in programs in which you want to provide more than two possible paths.

Do not include a semicolon at the end of the lines with expressions to be tested or on the line with the keyword else.

The syntax for writing a nested if statement in Java is as follows:

```
if(expressionA)
    statementA;
else if(expressionB)
    statementB;
else
    statementC;
```

This is called a nested if statement because the second if statement is a part of the first if statement. This is easier to see if the example is changed as follows:

```
if(expressionA)
    statementA;
else
    if(expressionB)
        statementB;
    else
        statementC;
```

Now let's see how a nested if statement works. As shown in Figure 4-3, if *expressionA* evaluates to true, then the computer executes *statementA*. If *expressionA* evaluates to false, then the computer will evaluate *expressionB*. If *expressionB* evaluates to true, then the computer will execute *statementB*. If both *expressionA* and *expressionB* evaluate to false, then the computer will execute *statementC*. Regardless of which path is taken in this code, the statement following the if-else statement is the next one to execute.

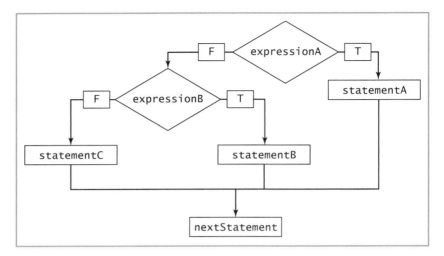

Figure 4-3   Evaluation of a nested `if` statement

The Java code sample that follows illustrates a nested `if` statement.

```java
if(empDept <= 3)
    supervisorName = "Dillon";
else if(empDept <= 7)
    supervisorName = "Escher";
else
    supervisorName = "Fontana";
System.out.println("Supervisor: " + supervisorName);
```

When you read the preceding code, you can assume that a department number is never less than 1. If the value of the variable named `empDept` is less than or equal to the value 3 (in the range of values from 1 to 3), then the value "Dillon" is assigned to the variable named `supervisorName`. If the value of `empDept` is not less than or equal to 3, but it is less than or equal to 7 (in the range of values from 4 to 7), then the value "Escher" is assigned to the variable named `supervisorName`. If the value of `empDept` is not in the range of values from 1 to 7, then the value "Fontana" is assigned to the variable named `supervisorName`. As you can see, there are three possible paths this program could take when the nested `if` statement is encountered. Regardless of which path the program takes, the next statement to execute is the output statement `System.out.println("Supervisor: " + supervisorName);`.

Exercise 4-3: Understanding Nested `if` Statements

In this exercise, you use what you have learned about writing nested `if` statements. This program was written for the Woof Wash dog-grooming business to calculate a total charge for services rendered. Woof Wash charges $20 for a bath, $10 for a trim cut, and $8 to clip nails. Study the following code and then answer Questions 1–3.

```java
// WoofWash.java - This program determines if a doggy
// service is provided and prints the charge.
import javax.swing.*; // import package javax.swing
public class WoofWash
{
    public static void main(String args [])
    {
        // This is the work done in the housekeeping() method
        String service;
        final String SERVICE_1 = "bath";
        final String SERVICE_2 = "cut";
        final String SERVICE_3 = "trim nails";
        double charge;
        final double BATH_CHARGE = 20.00;
        final double CUT_CHARGE = 10.00;
        final double NAIL_CHARGE = 8.00;
        service =
           JOptionPane.showInputDialog ("Enter service: ");
        // This is the work done in the detailLoop() method
        if(service.equals(SERVICE_1))
           charge = BATH_CHARGE;
        else if(service.equals(SERVICE_2))
           charge = CUT_CHARGE;
        else if(service.equals(SERVICE_3))
           charge = NAIL_CHARGE;
        else
           charge = 0.00;
        // This is the work done in the endOfJob() method
        if(charge > 0.00)
           System.out.println("The charge for a doggy " +
                        service + " is $" + charge + ".");
        else
           System.out.println("We do not perform the " +
                        service + " service.");
        System.exit (0);
    }
}
```

1. What is the exact output when this program executes if the user enters "bath"?

   _____

   _____

2. What is the exact output when this program executes if the user enters "shave"?

_____

_____

3. What is the exact output when this program executes if the nested if statement is changed to if(service == SERVICE_1) and the user enters "bath"?

_____

_____

LAB 4.3 Using Nested if Statements

In this lab, you complete a prewritten Java program that calculates an employee's end-of-year bonus and prints the employee's name, yearly salary, performance rating, and bonus. Bonuses are calculated based on an employee's annual salary and his or her performance rating. The rating system is contained in Table 4-4:

Rating	Bonus
1	15% of annual salary
2	10% of annual salary
3	6% of annual salary
4	None

Table 4-4   Employee ratings and bonuses

1. Open the file named EmployeeBonus.java using Notepad or the text editor of your choice.

2. Variables have been declared for you and the input statements and output statements have been written. Read them over carefully before you proceed to the next step.

3. Design the logic and write the rest of the program using a nested if statement.

4. Compile the program.

5. Execute the program entering the following as input:

    Employee's name: Laurie Blair
    Employee's salary: 65000.00
    Employee's performance rating: 3

6. Your output should be: Employee Name: Laurie Blair
Employee Salary: $65000.0
Employee Rating: 3
Employee Bonus: $3900.0

You cannot control the number of places that appear after the decimal point until you learn more about Java in Chapter 9 of this book.

The `switch` Statement

The `switch` statement is similar to a nested `if` statement because it is also a multipath decision statement. A `switch` statement offers the advantage of being easier for you to read than nested `if` statements, and a `switch` statement is also easier for you, the programmer, to maintain. You use the `switch` statement in situations when you want to compare an expression with several integer constants.

The syntax for writing a `switch` statement in Java is as follows:

```
switch(expression)
{
    case constant: statement(s);
    case constant: statement(s);
    case constant: statement(s);
    default:       statement(s);
}
```

If you omit a **break** statement in a **case**, all the code up to the next **break** statement or a closing curly brace is executed. This is probably not what you intend.

You begin writing a `switch` statement with the keyword `switch`. Then, within parentheses, you include an expression that evaluates to an integer value. Cases are then defined within the `switch` statement by using the keyword `case` as a label, and including an integer value after this label. For example, you could include an integer constant such as 10 or an arithmetic expression that evaluates to an integer such as 10/2. The computer evaluates the expression in the `switch` statement and then compares it to the integer values following the `case` labels. If the expression and the integer value match, then the computer executes the statement(s) that follow until it encounters a `break` statement or a closing curly brace. The `break` statement causes an exit from the `switch` statement. You can use the keyword `default` to establish a case for values that do not match any of the integer values following the `case` labels. Note also that all of the cases, including the default case, are enclosed within curly braces.

The following code sample illustrates the use of the `switch` statement in Java:

```
int deptNum;
String deptName;
deptNum = 2;
switch(deptNum)
{
    case 1:     deptName = "Marketing";
                break;
    case 2:     deptName = "Development";
                break;
    case 3:     deptName = "Sales";
                break;
    default:    deptName = "Unknown";
                break;
}
System.out.println("Department: " + deptName);
```

In the preceding example, when the program encounters the switch statement, the value of the variable named deptNum is 2. The value 2 matches the integer constant 2 in the second case of the switch statement. Therefore, the string constant "Development" is assigned to the String variable named deptName. A break statement is encountered next, and causes the program to exit from the switch statement. The statement following the switch statement System.out.println("Department: " + deptName); executes next.

Exercise 4-4: Using a switch Statement

In this exercise, you use what you have learned about the switch statement. Study the following code and then answer Questions 1–5.

```
int numValue = 20;
int answer = 0;
switch(numValue)
{
    case 10:    answer += 10;
    case 20:    answer += 20;
    case 30:    answer += 30;
                break;
    case 40:    answer += 40;
    case 50:    answer += 50;
    default:    answer = 0;
                break;
}
System.out.println("Answer: " + answer);
```

1. What is the value of answer if the value of numValue is 20?

_____

2. What is the value of answer if the value of numValue is 40?

_____

3. What is the value of answer if the value of numValue is 10?

_____

4. What is the value of answer if the value of numValue is 22?

_____

5. Is the break statement in the default case needed? Explain.

_____

LAB 4.4   Using a switch Statement

In this lab, you complete a prewritten Java program that calculates an employee's end-of-year bonus and prints the employee's name, yearly salary, performance rating, and bonus. This is the same program you wrote in Lab 4.3 when you used nested if statements to write the program. This time you use a switch statement instead of nested if statements.

In this program, bonuses are calculated based on employees' annual salary and their performance rating. The rating system is contained in Table 4-5:

Rating	Bonus
1	15% of annual salary
2	10% of annual salary
3	6% of annual salary
4	None

Table 4-5   Employee ratings and bonuses

1. Open the file named EmployeeBonus2.java using Notepad or the text editor of your choice.

2. Variables have been declared for you, and the input statements and output statements have been written. Read them over carefully before you proceed to the next step.

3. Design the logic and write the rest of the program using a switch statement.

4. Compile the program.

5. Execute the program entering the following as input:

Employee's name: Laurie Blair
Employee's salary: 65000.00
Employee's performance rating: 3

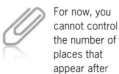

For now, you cannot control the number of places that appear after the decimal point. You will learn how to do this in Chapter 9 of this book.

6. Confirm that your output matches the following:

Employee Name: Laurie Blair
Employee Salary: $65000.0
Employee Rating: 3
Employee Bonus: $3900.0

Using Decision Statements to Make Multiple Comparisons

When you write programs, you must often write statements that include multiple comparisons. For example, you may want to determine that two conditions are **true** before you decide which path your program will take. In the next sections, you learn how to implement AND logic in a program by using the **&&** (AND) logical operator. You also learn how to implement OR logic using the **||** (OR) logical operator.

Using AND Logic

When you write Java programs, you can use the AND operator (**&&**) to make multiple comparisons in a single decision statement. Remember when using AND logic, that all expressions must evaluate to **true** for the entire expression to be **true**.

The Java code that follows illustrates a decision statement that uses the AND operator (**&&**) to implement AND logic:

```
String medicalPlan = "Y";
String dentalPlan = "Y";
if(medicalPlan.equals("Y") && dentalPlan.equals("Y"))
    System.out.println("Employee has medical insurance" +
                    " and also has dental insurance.");
else
    System.out.println("Employee may have medical" +
    " insurance or may have dental insurance," +
    " but does not have both medical and" +
    " dental insurance.");
```

In this example, the variables named medicalPlan and dentalPlan have both been initialized to the string constant "Y". When the expression medicalPlan.equals("Y") is evaluated, the result is **true**. When the expression dentalPlan.equals("Y") is evaluated, the result is also **true**. Because both expressions evaluate to **true**, the entire expression, `medicalPlan.equals("Y") && dentalPlan.equals("Y")`, evaluates to `true`. Because the entire expression is `true`, the output generated is "Employee has medical insurance and also has dental insurance."

If you initialize either of the variables, `medicalPlan` or `dentalPlan`, with a value other than "Y", then the expression `medicalPlan.equals("Y") && dentalPlan.equals("Y")` evaluates to `false`, and the output generated is "Employee may have medical insurance or may have dental insurance, but does not have both medical and dental insurance."

Using OR Logic

You can use OR logic when you want to make multiple comparisons in a single decision statement. Of course, you must remember when using OR logic that only one expression must evaluate to `true` for the entire expression to be `true`.

The Java code that follows illustrates a decision statement that uses the OR operator (||) to implement OR logic:

```
String medicalPlan = "Y";
String dentalPlan = "N";
if(medicalPlan.equals("Y") || dentalPlan.equals("Y"))
   System.out.println("Employee has medical insurance" +
               " or dental insurance or both.");
else
   System.out.println("Employee does not have medical" +
       " insurance and also does not have dental" +
       " insurance.");
```

In this example, the variable named `medicalPlan` is initialized with the string constant "Y", and the variable named `dentalPlan` is initialized to the string constant "N". When the expression `medicalPlan.equals("Y")` is evaluated, the result is `true`. When the expression `dentalPlan.equals("Y")` is evaluated, the result is `false`. The expression, `medicalPlan.equals("Y") || dentalPlan.equals("Y")`, evaluates to `true` because when using OR logic, only one of the expressions must evaluate to `true` for the entire expression to be `true`. Because the entire expression is `true`, the output generated is "Employee has medical insurance or dental insurance or both."

If you initialize both of the variables, `medicalPlan` and `dentalPlan`, with the string constant "N", then the expression, `medicalPlan.equals("Y") || dentalPlan.equals("Y")`, evaluates to `false`, and the output generated is "Employee does not have medical insurance and also does not have dental insurance."

Exercise 4-5: Making Multiple Comparisons in Decision Statements

In this exercise, you use what you have learned about OR logic. This example program was written for a marketing research firm that wants to determine if a customer prefers Coke or Pepsi over some other drink. Study the following code and then answer Questions 1–4.

```java
// CokeOrPepsi.java - This program determines if a
// customer prefers to drink Coke or Pepsi or some other
// drink.
import javax.swing.*;
public class CokeOrPepsi
{
    public static void main(String args[])
    {
        String customerName;  // Customer's name.
        String drink = " ";   // Customer's favorite drink.
        // This is the work done in the housekeeping() method
        customerName = JOptionPane.showInputDialog(
                            "Enter customer's name: ");
        drink = JOptionPane.showInputDialog(
                "Enter customer's drink preference: ");
        // This is the work done in the detailLoop() method
        if(drink.equals("Coke") || drink.equals("Pepsi"))
        {
            System.out.println("Customer Name: " +
                                customerName);
            System.out.println("Drink: " + drink);
        }
        else
            System.out.println(customerName +
                        " does not prefer Coke or Pepsi.");
        // This is the work done in the endOfJob() method
        System.exit(0);
    }
}
```

1. What is the exact output when this program executes if the customer's name is "Sally Preston" and the drink is "Pepsi"?

   _____

   _____

2. What is the exact output when this program executes if the customer's name is "Sally Preston" and the drink is "Coke"?

   _____

   _____

3. What is the exact output from this program when

   `if(drink.equals("Coke") || drink.equals("Pepsi"))`

   is changed to

   `if(drink.equals("Coke") && drink.equals("Pepsi"))`

   and the customer's name is still "Sally Preston" and the drink is still "Coke"?

   _____

   _____

4. What is the exact output from this program when

   `if(drink.equals("Coke") || drink.equals("Pepsi"))`

   is changed to

   `if(drink.equals("Coke") || drink.equals("Pepsi") ||`
   `    drink.equals("coke") || drink.equals("pepsi"))`

   and the customer's name is "Sally Preston", and the drink is "pepsi"? What does this change allow a user to enter?

   _____

   _____

LAB 4.5 Making Multiple Comparisons in Decision Statements

In this lab, you complete a partially written Java program for an airline that offers a 10% discount to passengers who are 12 years old or younger and the same discount to passengers who are 65 years old or older. The program should request a passenger's name and age, and then print whether the passenger is eligible or not eligible for a discount.

1. Open the file named `Airline.java` using Notepad or the text editor of your choice.

2. Variables have been declared and initialized for you, and the input statements have been written. Read them carefully before you proceed to the next step.

3. Design the logic deciding whether to use AND or OR logic. Write the decision statement to identify when a discount should be offered and when a discount should not be offered.

4. Be sure to include output statements telling whether or not the customer is eligible for a discount.

5. Compile the program.

6. Execute the program, entering the following as input:

   a. Customer Name: Connie Chen
      Customer Age : 22
      What is the output? _____

   b. Customer Name: William Gorman
      Customer Age : 66
      What is the output? _____

   c. Customer Name: Maria Gonzales
      Customer Age : 72
      What is the output? _____

   d. Customer Name: Sheila Morton
      Customer Age : 52
      What is the output? _____

   e. Customer Name: Timmy Morton
      Customer Age : 2
      What is the output? _____

   f. Customer Name: Helen Patel
      Customer Age : 12
      What is the output? _____

Writing Programs Using Loops

After studying this chapter, you will be able to:

- ◎ Use Java's increment (++) and decrement (--) operators
- ◎ Recognize how and when to use `while` loops in Java, including how to use a counter and how to use a sentinel value to control a loop
- ◎ Use `for` loops in Java
- ◎ Write a `do while` loop in Java
- ◎ Include nested loops in applications
- ◎ Accumulate totals by using a loop in a Java application
- ◎ Use a loop to validate user input in an application

In this chapter, you learn how to use Java to program three types of loops: a `while` loop, a `do while` loop, and a `for` loop. You also learn how to nest loops, how to use a loop to help you accumulate a total in your programs, and how to use a loop to validate user input. You should do the exercises and labs in this chapter only after you have finished Chapter 5 in your book, *Programming Logic and Design, Sixth Edition*. In that chapter, you learned that loops change the flow of control in a program by allowing a programmer to direct the computer to execute a statement or a group of statements multiple times. But before you start learning about Java's loops, it is helpful to learn about two additional operators, the increment and decrement operators.

The Increment (++) and Decrement (−−) Operators

You will often use the increment and decrement operators when your programs require loops. These operators provide a concise, efficient method for adding 1 to (incrementing) or subtracting 1 from (decrementing) an lvalue. An **lvalue** is an area of memory in which a value your program needs may be stored. In Java code, you place an lvalue on the left side of an assignment statement. Recall that an assignment statement stores a value at a memory location that is associated with a variable, and you place a variable name on the left side of an assignment statement.

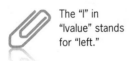

The "l" in "lvalue" stands for "left."

For example, the Java assignment statement:

```
number = 10;
```

assigns the value 10 to the variable named `number`. This causes the computer to store the value 10 at the memory location associated with `number`. Because the increment and decrement operators add 1 to or subtract 1 from an lvalue, the statement `number++;` is equivalent to `number = number + 1;` and the statement `number--;` is equivalent to `number = number - 1;`. Each expression changes or writes to the memory location associated with the variable named `number`.

Both the increment and decrement operators have prefix and postfix forms. Which form you use depends on when you want to increment or decrement the value stored in the variable. When you use the prefix form, as in `++number`, you place the operator in front of the name of the variable. This increments or decrements the lvalue immediately. When you use the postfix form, as in `number++`, you place the operator after the name of the variable. This increments or decrements the lvalue after it is used.

The example that follows illustrates the use of both forms of the increment operator in Java.

```
x = 5;
y = x++;   // Postfix form
           // y is assigned the value of x,
           // then x is incremented.
           // Value of x is 6.
           // Value of y is 5.
x = 5;
y = ++x;   // Prefix form
           // x is incremented first, then
           // the value of x is assigned to y.
           // Value of x is 6.
           // Value of y is 6.
```

You might understand the postfix form better if you think of the statement y = x++; as being the same as the following:

```
x = 5;
y = x;
x = x + 1;
```

To understand the prefix form better, think of y = ++x; as being the same as the following:

```
x = 5;
x = x + 1;
y = x;
```

Exercise 5-1: Using the Increment (++) and Decrement (--) Operators

In this exercise, you use what you have learned about Java's increment and decrement operators to answer Questions 1–4.

1. Examine the following code:

   ```
   x = 3;
   y = ++x;
   ```

   After this code executes, what is the value of x? _____
   y? _____

2. Examine the following code:

   ```
   x = 3;
   y = x++;
   ```

   After this code executes, what is the value of x? _____
   y? _____

3. Examine the following code:

```
x = 3;
y = --x;
```

After this code executes, what is the value of x? _____

y? _____

4.   Examine the following code:

```
x = 3;
y = x--;
```

After this code executes, what is the value of x? _____

y? _____

Writing a `while` Loop in Java

As you learned in *Programming Logic and Design, Sixth Edition*, three steps must occur in every loop:

1.   You must initialize a variable that will control the loop. This variable is known as the **loop control variable**.

2.   You must compare the loop control variable to some value, known as the **sentinel value**, which decides whether the loop continues or stops. This decision is based on a Boolean comparison. The result of a Boolean comparison is always a `true` or `false` value.

3.   Within the loop, you must alter the value of the loop control variable.

Remember that a block statement is several statements within a pair of curly braces.

You also learned that the statements that are part of a loop are referred to as the **loop body**. In Java, the loop body may consist of a single statement or a block statement.

The statements that make up the loop body may be any type of statements, including assignment statements, decision statements, or even other loops. Note that the Java syntax for writing a `while` loop is as follows:

```
while(expression)
    statement;
```

Notice that there is no semicolon after the ending parenthesis. Placing a semicolon after the ending parenthesis is not a syntax error, but it is a logic error. It results in an **infinite** loop, which is a loop that never stops executing the statements in its body. It never stops executing because the semicolon is a statement called the **null** statement and is interpreted as "do nothing." Think of a `while` loop with a semicolon after the ending parenthesis as meaning "while the condition is true, do nothing forever."

The while loop allows you to direct the computer to execute the statement in the body of the loop as long as the expression within the parentheses evaluates to **true**. Study the example that follows, which illustrates a while loop that uses a block statement as its loop body:

```
final int NUM_TIMES = 3;
num = 0;
while(num < NUM_TIMES)
{
    System.out.println("Welcome to Java Programming.");
    num++;
}
```

In this example, a block statement is used because the loop body contains more than one statement.

The first statement causes the text "Welcome to Java Programming." to appear on the user's screen. The second statement, num++;, is important because it causes num, the loop control variable, to be incremented. When the loop is first encountered, the comparison, num < NUM_TIMES, is made for the first time when the value of num is 0. The 0 is compared to, and found to be less than, 3, which means the condition is **true**, and the text "Welcome to Java Programming." is displayed for the first time. The next statement, num++;, causes 1 to be added to the value of num. The second time the comparison is made, the value of num is 1, which is still less than 3, and causes the text to appear a second time followed by adding 1 to the value of num. The third comparison also results in a **true** value because the value of num is now 2, and 2 is still less than 3; as a result, the text appears a third time, and num is incremented again. The fourth time the comparison is made, the value of num is 3, which is not less than 3; as a result, the program exits the loop.

The loop in the next code example produces the same results as the previous example. The text "Welcome to Java Programming." is displayed three times.

```
final int NUM_TIMES = 3;
num = 0;
while(num++ < NUM_TIMES)
    System.out.println("Welcome to Java Programming.");
```

Be sure you understand why the postfix increment operator is used in the expression num++ < NUM_TIMES.

The first time this comparison is made, the value of num is 0. The 0 is then compared to, and found to be less than, 3, which means the condition is **true**, and the text "Welcome to Java Programming." is displayed.

The second time the comparison is made, the value of num is 1; because 1 is still less than 3, the text appears a second time. The third comparison also results in a **true** value because the value of num is

 When you use the postfix increment operator, the value of **num** is not incremented until after the comparison is made.

now 2, and 2 is still less than 3; as a result, the text appears a third time. The fourth time the comparison is made, the value of num is 3, which is not less than 3; as a result, the program exits the loop.

If the prefix increment operator is used in the expression ++num < NUM_TIMES, the loop executes twice instead of three times. This occurs because the first time this comparison is made, num is incremented before the comparison is done. This results in num having a value of 1 the first time "Welcome to Java Programming." is displayed and a value of 2 the second time it is displayed. Then, when the value of num is 3, the condition is false, causing the program to exit the loop. This time, "Welcome to Java Programming." is not displayed.

It is important to understand the difference between the prefix and postfix forms of the increment and decrement operators.

Exercise 5-2: Using a while Loop

In this exercise, you use what you have learned about writing while loops. Study the following code and then answer Questions 1–4.

```
final int NUM_LOOPS = 7;
int numberOfTimes = NUM_LOOPS;
while(numberOfTimes++ < NUM_LOOPS)
    System.out.println("Value of numberOfTimes is " +
                            numberOfTimes);
```

1. What is the loop control variable?

    _____

2. What is the output?

    _____

3. What is the output if the code is changed to
    while(numberOfTimes++ <= NUM_LOOPS)?

    _____

4. What is the output if the code is changed to
    while(++numberOfTimes <= NUM_LOOPS)?

    _____

Using a Counter to Control a Loop

In Chapter 5 of *Programming Logic and Design, Sixth Edition*, you learned that you can use a counter to control a while loop. With a counter, you set up the loop to execute a specified number of times. Also recall that a while loop will execute zero times if the expression used in the comparison immediately evaluates to false. In that case, the computer does not execute the body of the loop at all.

Chapter 5 of *Programming Logic and Design, Sixth Edition* discusses a counter-controlled loop that controls how many times the word "Hello" is printed. Let's take a look at the following pseudocode for this counter-controlled loop:

```
start
   Declarations
      num count = 0
   while count < 4
      print "Hello"
      count = count + 1
   endwhile
         output "Goodbye"
   stop
```

The counter for this loop is a variable named count, which is assigned the value 0. The Boolean expression, count < 4, is tested to see if the value of count is less than 4. If true, the loop executes. If false, the program exits the loop. If the loop executes, the program displays the word "Hello", and then adds 1 to the value of count. Given this pseudocode, the loop body executes four times, and the word "Hello" is displayed four times.

Incrementing the counter variable is an important statement. Each time through the loop, the count variable must be incremented or the expression, count < 4, would never be false. This would result in an infinite loop.

Now, let's see what the code looks like when you translate the pseudocode to Java:

```java
int count = 0;
while(count < 4)
{
    System.out.println("Hello");
    count++;
}
```

First, the variable count is assigned a value of 0 and is used as the counter variable to control the while loop. The while loop follows and includes the Boolean expression, count < 4, within parentheses. The counter-controlled loop executes a block statement that is marked by an opening curly brace and a closing curly brace. The statements in the loop body display the word "Hello" and then increment count, which adds 1 to the counter variable.

Exercise 5-3: Using a Counter-Controlled while Loop

In this exercise, you use what you have learned about counter-controlled loops. Study the following code and then answer Questions 1–4.

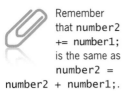

Remember that number2 += number1; is the same as number2 = number2 + number1;.

```
number1 = 0;
number2 = 0;
while(number1 < 8)
    number1++;
    number2 += number1;
```

1. What is the value of number1 when the loop exits?

_____

2. What is the value of number2 when the loop exits?

_____

3. If the statement number1++ is changed to ++number1, what is the value of number1 when the loop exits?

_____

4. What could you do to force the value of number2 to be 36 when the loop exits?

_____

LAB 5.1   Using a Counter-Controlled while Loop

In this lab, you use a counter-controlled while loop in a Java program provided with the data files for this book. When completed, the program should print the numbers 0 through 10, along with their values doubled and quadrupled (multiplied by four). The data file contains the necessary variable declarations and output statements.

1. Open the source code file named DoubleQuadruple.java using Notepad or the text editor of your choice.

2. Write a counter-controlled while loop that uses the loop control variable to take on the values 0 through 10. Remember to initialize the loop control variable before the program enters the loop.

3. In the body of the loop, calculate the double and the quadruple using the value of the loop control variable. Remember to change the value of the loop control variable in the body of the loop.

4. Save the source code file in a directory of your choice, and then make that directory your working directory.

5. Compile the source code file, DoubleQuadruple.java.

6. Execute the program. Record the output of this program.

_____

_____

Using a Sentinel Value to Control a Loop

As you learned in Chapter 1 of *Programming Logic and Design, Sixth Edition*, a sentinel value is a value such as "Y" or "N" that a user must supply to stop a loop. To learn about sentinel values in Java, we will look at a program discussed in Chapter 5 of *Programming Logic and Design, Sixth Edition* and in Chapter 3 of this book. The program creates a payroll report for a small company. This program includes a `while` loop and uses a sentinel value to determine when the loop executes or when the loop is exited. The pseudocode is shown below.

```
start
   Declarations
      string name
      num gross
      num deduct
      num net
      num RATE = 0.25
      string QUIT = "XXX"
      string REPORT_HEADING = "Payroll Report""
      string COLUMN_HEADING = "Name   Gross   Deductions   Net"
      string END_LINE = "**End of report"
   housekeeping()
   while not name = QUIT
      detailLoop()
   endwhile
   endOfJob()
stop

housekeeping()
   output REPORT_HEADING
   output COLUMN_HEADING
   input name
return

detailLoop()
   input gross
   deduct = gross * RATE
   net = gross - deduct
   output name, gross, deduct, net
   input name
return

endOfJob()
   output END_LINE
return
```

Figure 5-1   Pseudocode for a payroll report program

Note that a **priming read** is included in the housekeeping() method in the pseudocode shown in Figure 5-1. Recall that you perform a priming read before a loop executes to input a value that is then used to control the loop. When a priming read is used, the program must perform another read within the loop body to get the next input value. You can see the priming read, the loop, and the last output statement portion of the pseudocode translated to Java in the following code sample:

```java
name = JOptionPane.showInputDialog(
        "Enter employee's name or XXX to quit: ");

while(name.compareTo(QUIT) != 0)
{
    // This is the work done in the detailLoop() method
    grossString = JOptionPane.showInputDialog(
                    "Enter employee's gross pay: ");
    gross = Double.parseDouble(grossString);
    deduct = gross * RATE;
    net = gross - deduct;
    System.out.println("Name: " + name);
    System.out.println("Gross Pay: " + gross);
    System.out.println("Deductions: " + deduct);
    System.out.println("Net Pay: " + net);
    name = JOptionPane.showInputDialog(
            "Enter employee's name or XXX to quit: ");
}
// This is the work done in the endOfJob() method
System.out.println(END_LINE);
```

In this code example, the variable named name is the loop control variable. It is assigned a value when the program instructs the user to "Enter employee's name or XXX to quit: " and reads the user's response. The loop control variable is tested with name.compareTo(QUIT) != 0. If the user enters a name (any value other than "XXX", which is the constant value of QUIT), then the test expression is true and the statements within the loop body execute. If the user enters "XXX" (the constant value of QUIT), which is the sentinel value, then the test expression is false, and the loop is exited.

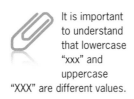
It is important to understand that lowercase "xxx" and uppercase "XXX" are different values.

The first statement instructs the user to enter an employee's gross pay. The program then retrieves the user's input and stores it in the String variable named grossString and then coverts the String to a Double and stores it in the variable named gross. The employee's deductions are calculated next and stored in the variable named deduct followed by the program calculating the employee's net pay and storing the value in the variable named net. Next, the program outputs the name of the employee followed by the employee's gross pay, deductions, and net pay.

The last statement in the loop prompts the user for a new value for name. This is the statement that changes the value of the loop control variable. The loop body ends when program control returns to the top of the loop, where the Boolean expression in the while statement is tested again. If the user enters the next employee's name at the last prompt, then the loop is entered again, and a new gross pay is input followed by calculations that determine new values for deductions and net pay. Next, the program displays the name of the employee followed by this employee's gross pay, deductions, and net pay. The program then prompts the user to enter a new value for name. If the user enters "XXX", then the test expression is false, and the loop body doesn't execute. When the loop is exited, the next statement to execute displays "**End of Report" (the constant value of END_LINE).

Exercise 5-4: Using a Sentinel Value to Control a while Loop

In this exercise, you use what you have learned about sentinel values. Study the following code and then answer Questions 1–5.

```
stringNumToPrint = JOptionPane.showInputDialog(
    "How many pages do you want to print?");
numToPrint = Integer.parseInt(stringNumToPrint);
counter = 1;
while(counter <= numToPrint);
{
    System.out.println("Page Number " + counter);
    counter++;
}
System.out.println("Value of counter is " + counter);
```

1. What is the output if the user enters an 8?

    _____

2. What is the problem with this code, and how can you fix it?

    _____

3. Assuming you fix the problem, if the user enters 100 as the number of pages to print, what is the value of counter when the loop exits?

    _____

4. Assuming you fix the problem, if the user enters 0 as the number of pages to print, how many pages will print?

    _____

5. Assume you have fixed the problem discussed in Questions 2–4, and then you delete the curly braces. Now, what is the output if the user enters an 8 as the number of pages to print?

    _____

LAB 5.2   Using a Sentinel Value to Control a while Loop

In this lab, you write a while loop that uses a sentinel value to control a loop in a Java program provided with the data files for this book. You also write the statements that make up the body of the loop. The source code file already contains the necessary variable declarations and output statements. When completed, the program should print a payoff schedule for a credit card company customer. At the beginning of every month, 1.2% interest is added to the balance, and then the customer makes a payment equal to 5% of the current balance. When the balance reaches $10.00 or less, the customer can pay off the account. As you will see, this program generates a lot of output, even for one customer.

1. Open the source code file named Payoff.java using Notepad or the text editor of your choice.

2. Write the while loop using a sentinel value to control the loop, and also write the statements that make up the body of the loop.

3. Save this source code file in a directory of your choice, and then make that directory your working directory.

4. Compile the source code file, Payoff.java.

5. Execute the program. Input the following:

   Account Number: 6789A
   Customer Name: Jeanne Johnson
   Balance: 120.00

6. Record the final balance amount when the loan may be paid off.

Writing a for Loop in Java

In Chapter 5 of *Programming Logic and Design, Sixth Edition*, you learned that a for loop is a **definite** loop; this means this type of loop will execute a definite number of times. The following is the syntax for a for loop in Java:

```
for(expression1; expression2; expression3)
    statement;
```

In Java, the for loop consists of three expressions that are separated by semicolons and enclosed within parentheses. The for loop executes as follows:

- The first time the for loop is encountered, the first expression is evaluated. Usually, this expression initializes a variable that is used to control the for loop.

- Next, the second expression is evaluated. If the second expression evaluates to true, the loop statement executes. If the second expression evaluates to false, the loop is exited.

- After the loop statement executes, the third expression is evaluated. The third expression usually increments or decrements the variable that you initialized in the first expression.

- After the third expression is evaluated, the second expression is evaluated again. If the second expression still evaluates to true, the loop statement executes again, and then the third expression is evaluated again.

- This process continues until the second expression evaluates to false.

The following code sample illustrates a Java for loop. Notice that the code uses a block statement in the for loop.

```
int number = 0;
int count;
final int NUM_LOOPS = 10;
for(count = 0; count < NUM_LOOPS; count++)
{
    number += count;
    System.out.println("Value of number is: " + number);
}
```

In this for loop example, the variable named count is initialized to 0 in the first expression. The second expression is a Boolean expression that evaluates to true or false. When the expression count < NUM_LOOPS is evaluated the first time, the value of count is 0 and the result is true. The loop body is then entered. This is where a new value is computed and assigned to the variable named number and then is displayed. The first time through the loop, the output is as follows: Value of number is: 0.

After the output is displayed, the third expression in the for loop is evaluated; this adds 1 to the value of count, making the new value of count equal to 1. When expression two is evaluated a second time, the value of count is 1. The program then tests to see if the value of count is less than NUM_LOOPS. This results in a true value and causes the loop body to execute again where a new value is computed for number and then displayed. The second time through the loop, the output is as follows: Value of number is: 1.

Next, expression three is evaluated; this adds 1 to the value of count. The value of count is now 2. Expression two is evaluated a third time and again is true because 2 is less than NUM_LOOPS. The third time through, the loop body changes the value of number to 3 and then displays the new value. The output is as follows: Value of number is: 3.

This process continues until the value of count becomes 10. At this time, 10 is not less than NUM_LOOPS, so the second expression results in a false value, and causes an exit from the for loop.

The counter-controlled loop that displays the word "Hello" four times (which you studied in the "Using a Counter to Control a Loop" section of this chapter) can be rewritten using a for loop instead of the while loop. In fact, when you know how many times a loop will execute, it is considered a good programming practice to use a for loop instead of a while loop.

To rewrite the while loop as a for loop, you can delete the assignment statement, counter = 0; because you initialize counter in expression one. You can also delete counter++; from the loop body because you increment counter in expression three. The program continues to print the word "Hello" in the body of the loop. The following code sample illustrates this for loop:

The curly braces are not required because now the loop body contains just one statement. However, it is good programming practice to include them, as it makes the code more readable and may help prevent an error later if additional statements are added to the body of the loop.

```
int counter;
final int NUM_LOOPS = 4;
for(counter = 0; counter < NUM_LOOPS; counter++)
{
    System.out.println("Hello");
}
```

Exercise 5-5: Using a for Loop

In this exercise, you use what you have learned about for loops. Study the following code and then answer Questions 1–4.

```
final int NUM_LOOPS = 26;
int numTimes;
for(numTimes = 1; numTimes <= NUM_LOOPS; numTimes++)
{
    System.out.println("Value of numTimes is: " + numTimes);
    numTimes++;
}
```

Answer the following four questions with "True" or "False."

1. This loop executes 26 times.

2. This loop could be written as a while loop.

   _____

3. Changing the <= operator to < will make no difference in the output.

   _____

4. This loop executes 13 times.

   _____

LAB 5.3   Using a for Loop

In this lab, you work with the same Java program you worked with in Lab 5.1. As in Lab 5.1, the completed program should print the numbers 0 through 10, along with their values doubled and quadrupled. However, in this lab, you should accomplish this using a for loop instead of a counter-controlled while loop.

1. Open the source code file named NewDoubleQuadruple.java using Notepad or the text editor of your choice.

2. Write a for loop that uses the loop control variable to take on the values 0 through 10.

3. In the body of the loop, calculate the double and the quadruple using the value of the loop control variable.

4. Save this source code file in a directory of your choice, and then make that directory your working directory.

5. Compile the source code file, NewDoubleQuadruple.java.

6. Execute the program. Is the output the same?

Writing a do while Loop in Java

In Chapter 5 of *Programming Logic and Design, Sixth Edition*, you learned about the do-until loop. Java does not support a do-until loop, but it does have a do while loop. The do while loop uses logic that can be stated as "do a while b is true." This is similar to a while loop; however, there is a difference. When you use a while loop, the condition is tested before the statements in the loop body execute. When you use a do while loop, the condition is tested after the statements in the loop body execute once. As a result, you should choose a do while loop when your program logic requires the body of the loop to execute at least once. The body of a do while loop continues to execute as long as the expression evaluates to true. The do while syntax is as follows:

```
do
    statement;
while(expression);
```

The following do while loop is a revised version of the while loop you saw earlier, which prints the word "Hello" four times. In this version, the loop is rewritten as a do while loop.

```
counter = 0;
final int NUM_LOOPS = 4;
do
{
    System.out.println("Hello");
    counter++;
} while(counter < NUM_LOOPS);
```

In this example, notice that you use block statements in do while loops just as in while and for loops. When this loop is entered, the word "Hello" is printed, the value of counter is incremented, and then the value of counter is compared with the constant NUM_LOOPS. Notice that the word "Hello" will always be printed at least once because the loop control variable, counter, is compared to NUM_LOOPS at the bottom of the loop.

Exercise 5-6: Using a do while Loop

In this exercise, you use what you have learned about do while loops. Study the following code and then answer Questions 1–4.

```
final int NUM_TIMES = 3;
int loopNum = 0;
do
{
    loopNum++;
    System.out.println("Strike " + loopNum);
}while(loopNum < NUM_TIMES);
```

1. How many times does this loop execute?

   _____

2. What is the output of this program?

   _____

3. Is the output different if you change the order of the statements in the body of the loop, so that loopNum++ comes after the output statement?

   _____

4. What is the loop control variable?

_____

LAB 5.4 Using a do while Loop

In this lab, you work with the same Java program you worked with in Labs 5.1 and 5.3. As in those earlier labs, the completed program should print the numbers 0 through 10, along with their values doubled and quadrupled. However, in this lab you should accomplish this using a do while loop.

By revising the same file three different ways in this chapter, you have seen that a single problem can be solved in different ways.

1. Open the source code file named NewestDoubleQuadruple.java using Notepad or the text editor of your choice.

2. Write a do while loop that uses the loop control variable to take on the values 0 through 10.

3. In the body of the loop, calculate the double and the quadruple using the value of the loop control variable.

4. Save this source code file in a directory of your choice, and then make that directory your working directory.

5. Compile the source code file, NewestDoubleQuadruple.java.

6. Execute the program. Is the output the same?

Nesting Loops

As the logic of your programs becomes more complex, you may find that you need to use nested loops. That is, you may need to include a loop within another loop. You have learned that when you use nested loops in a program, you must use multiple control variables to control the separate loops.

In Chapter 5 of *Programming Logic and Design, Sixth Edition*, you studied the design logic for a program that produces a quiz answer sheet. Some of the declarations and a section of the pseudocode for this program are as follows:

```
num PARTS = 5
num QUESTIONS = 3
string PART_LABEL = "Part "
sting LINE = ". _____"
string QUIT = "ZZZ"
output quizName
```

```
partCounter = 1
while partCounter <= PARTS
   output PART_LABEL, partCounter
   questionCounter = 1
   while questionCounter <= QUESTIONS
      output questionCounter, LINE
      questionCounter = questionCounter + 1
   endwhile
   partCounter = partCounter + 1
endwhile
output "Enter next quiz name or ", QUIT, " to quit"
input quizName
```

This pseudocode includes two loops. The outer loop uses the loop control variable, partCounter, to control the loop using the sentinel value, 5 (constant value of PARTS). The inner loop uses the control variable questionCounter to keep track of the number of lines to print for the questions in a part of the quiz. Refer to Chapter 5 in *Programming Logic and Design, Sixth Edition* for a line-by-line description of the pseudocode. When you are sure you understand the logic, take a look at the code sample that follows. This code sample shows some of the Java code for the Answer Sheet program.

```java
int partCounter;
int questionCounter;
final int PARTS = 5;
final int QUESTIONS = 3;
final String PART_LABEL = "Part ";
final String LINE = ". _____";
partCounter = 1;
while(partCounter <= PARTS)
{
   System.out.println(PART_LABEL + partCounter);
   questionCounter = 1;
   while(questionCounter <= QUESTIONS)
   {
      System.out.println(questionCounter + LINE);
      questionCounter++;
   }
   partCounter++;
}
```

The entire Java program is saved in a file named AnswerSheet.java. This file is included with the data files for this book. You may want to study the source code, compile it, and execute the program to experience how nested loops behave.

Exercise 5-7: Nesting Loops

In this exercise, you use what you have learned about nesting loops. Study the following code and then answer Questions 1–4.

```
int sum = 0;
final int MAX_ROWS = 5, MAX_COLS = 4;
int rows, columns;
for(rows = 0; rows < MAX_ROWS; rows++)
    for(columns = 0; columns < MAX_COLS; columns++)
        sum += rows + columns;
System.out.println("Value of sum is " + sum);
```

1. How many times does the outer loop execute?

   _____

2. How many times does the inner loop execute?

   _____

3. What is the value of sum printed by System.out.println()?

   _____

4. What would happen if you changed rows++ and columns++ to
   ++rows and ++columns?

   _____

LAB 5.5   Nesting Loops

In this lab, you add nested loops to a Java program provided with the data files for this book. The program should
print the outline of a rectangle, as shown in Figure 5-2. The
rectangle is printed using asterisks, four across and six down. Note
that this program uses System.out.print("*"); to print an asterisk
without a new line.

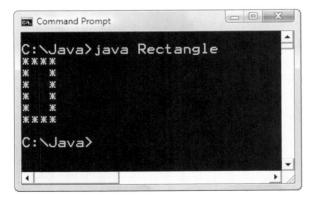

Figure 5-2   Rectangle printed by the Rectangle program

1. Open the source code file named Rectangle.java using
   Notepad or the text editor of your choice.

2. Write the nested loops to control the number of rows and the number of columns that make up the rectangle.

3. In the loop body, use a nested `if` statement to decide when to print an asterisk and when to print a space. The output statements have been written, but you must decide when and where to use them.

4. Save this source code file in a directory of your choice, and then make that directory your working directory.

5. Compile the source code file, `Rectangle.java`.

6. Execute the program. Your rectangle outline should look like the rectangle outline in Figure 5-2.

7. Modify the program to change the number of rows from six to eight and the number of columns from four to 10. What does the rectangle look like now?

Accumulating Totals in a Loop

You can use a loop in Java to accumulate a total as your program executes. For example, assume that your computer science instructor has asked you to design and write a program that she can use to calculate an average score for the midterm exam she gave last week. To find the average test score, you need to add all the students' test scores, and then divide that sum by the number of students who took the midterm.

Note that the logic for this program should include a loop that will execute for each student in the class. In the loop, you get a student's test score as input and add that value to a total. After you get all of the test scores and accumulate the sum of all the test scores, you divide that sum by the number of students. You should plan to ask the user to input the number of student test scores that will be entered, because your instructor wants to reuse this program using a different number of students each time it is executed.

As you review your work, you realize that the program will accumulate a sum within the loop and that you will also need to keep a count for the number of students. You learned in *Programming Logic and Design, Sixth Edition* that you add 1 to a counter each time a loop executes and that you add some other value to an accumulator. For this program, that other value added to the accumulator is a student's test score.

The following Java code sample shows the loop required for this program. Notice that the loop body includes an accumulator and a counter.

```java
// Get user input to control loop.
stringNum = JOptionPane.showInputDialog(
            "Enter number of students: ");
// Convert number String to int.
numStudents = Integer.parseInt(stringNum);
// Initialize accumulator variable to 0.
testTotal = 0;
// Loop for each student.
for(stuCount = 0; stuCount < numStudents; stuCount++)
{
    // Input student test score.
    stringScore = JOptionPane.showInputDialog(
                "Enter student's score: ");
    // Convert to integer.
    testScore = Integer.parseInt(stringScore);
    // Accumulate total of test scores.
    testTotal += testScore;
}
// Calculate average test score.
average = testTotal / stuCount;
```

If `testTotal` is not initialized, it will contain an unknown value referred to as a "garbage" value. In Java, your program will not compile if `testTotal` is not initialized.

You must calculate the average outside of the loop, not inside the loop. The only way to calculate the average inside the loop is to do it each time the loop executes, but this is inefficient.

If a user entered a 0, meaning 0 students took the midterm, the `for` loop would not execute because the value of `numStudents` is 0, and the value of `stuCount` is also 0.

In the code, you use the `showInputDialog()` method to ask your user to tell you how many students took the test. Then the program converts the `String` value that is returned by the `showInputDialog()` method to an `int` so that the value can be used in arithmetic calculations. Next, the accumulator, `testTotal`, is initialized to 0.

After the accumulator is initialized, the code uses a `for` loop and the loop control variable, `stuCount`, to control the loop. A `for` loop is a good choice because, at this point in the program, you know how many times the loop should execute. You use the `for` loop's first expression to initialize `stuCount`, and then the second expression is evaluated to see if `stuCount` is less than `numStudents`. If this is `true`, the body of the loop executes, displaying the `showInputDialog()` method again, this time asking the user to enter a test score.

As you examine the code, note that because the `showInputDialog()` method returns the `String` version of the value entered by the user, the program must convert this `String` to an `int` by using the `parseInt()` method. Then, you must add the value of `testScore` to the accumulator, `testTotal`. The loop control variable, `stuCount`, is then incremented, and the incremented value is tested to see if it is less than numStudents. If this is true again, the loop executes a second time. The loop continues to execute until the value of stuCount < numStudents is false. Outside the for loop, the program calculates the average test score by dividing testTotal by stuCount.

The entire Java program is saved in a file named TestAverage.java. You may want to study the source code, compile it, and execute the program to experience how accumulators and counters behave.

Exercise 5-8: Accumulating Totals in a Loop

In this exercise, you use what you have learned about using counters and accumulating totals in a loop. Study the following code and then answer Questions 1–4. The complete program is saved in the file named Rainfall.java. You may want to compile and execute the program to help you answer these questions.

```java
for(counter = 1; counter <= DAYS_IN_WEEK; counter++)
{
   stringRain = JOptionPane.showInputDialog(
      "Enter rainfall amount for Day " + counter);
   rainfall = Double.parseDouble(stringRain);
   System.out.println("Day " + counter +
      "rainfall amount is " + rainfall + " inches");
   sum += rainfall;
}
// calculate average
average = sum / DAYS_IN_WEEK;
```

1. What happens when you compile this program if the variable sum is not initialized with the value 0?

2. Could you replace sum += rainfall; with sum = sum + rainfall;?

3. The variables sum and average should be declared to be what data type to calculate the most accurate average rainfall?

4. Could you replace DAYS_IN_WEEK in the statement average = sum / DAYS_IN_WEEK; with the variable named counter and still get the desired result? Explain.

LAB 5.6 **Accumulating Totals in a Loop**

In this lab, you add a loop and the statements that make up the loop body to a Java program provided with the data files for this book. When completed, the program should calculate the total daily sales for a book store. Your loop should execute until the user enters the word "done" instead of a book title. After the user enters a book title, he or she should be asked to enter the transaction amount. The transaction amounts are listed in Table 5-1.

Book Title	Transaction Amount ($)
The Lost Symbol	29.95
The Time Traveler's Wife	14.95
The Weight of Silence	13.95
The White Queen	25.99
My Life in France	15.00
Three Cups of Tea	15.00
Outliers	27.99

Table 5-1   Input for Lab 5.6

When entering this data, take care not to type the dollar sign ($).

Note that variables have been declared for you, and the input and output statements have been written, but you must decide where they belong in the program.

1. Open the source code file named BookSales.java using Notepad or the text editor of your choice.

2. Write a loop and a loop body that allows you to calculate a total of daily sales for the bookstore.

3. Save this source code file in a directory of your choice, and then make that directory your working directory.

4. Compile the source code file, BookSales.java.

5. Execute the program using the data listed in Table 5-1. Record the output of this program.

_____

_____

_____

Using a Loop to Validate Input

In Chapter 5 of *Programming Logic and Design, Sixth Edition*, you learned that you cannot count on users to enter valid data in programs that ask them to enter data. You also learned that you should validate input from your user so you can avoid problems caused by invalid input.

If your program requires a user to enter a specific value, such as "Y" or "N", in response to a question, then your program should validate that your user entered an exact match to either "Y" or "N". You must also decide what action to take in your program if the user's input is not either "Y" or "N". As an example of testing for an exact match, consider the following code:

```
String answer;
answer = JOptionPane.showInputDialog(
        "Do you want to continue? Enter Y or N.");
while((answer.compareTo("Y") != 0) &&
      (answer.compareTo("N") != 0))
{
    answer =
      JOptionPane.showInputDialog(
      "Invalid Response. Please type Y or N.");
}
```

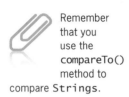 Remember that you use the compareTo() method to compare Strings.

In the example, the variable named answer contains your user's answer to the question "Do you want to continue? Enter Y or N.". In the expression that is part of the while loop, the program uses the compareTo() method to see if your user really did enter "Y" or "N". If not, the program enters the loop, telling the user he or she entered invalid input and then requesting that he or she type "Y" or "N". The expression in the while loop is tested again to see if the user entered valid data this time. If not, the loop body executes again and continues to execute until the user enters valid input.

You can also verify user input in a program that requests a user to enter numeric data. For example, your program could ask a user to enter a number in the range of 1 to 4. It is very important to verify this numeric input, especially if your program uses the input in arithmetic calculations. What would happen if the user entered the word "one" instead of the number 1? Or, what would happen if the user entered 100? More than likely, your program would not run correctly. The following code example illustrates how you can verify that a user enters correct numeric data.

```
String stringAnswer;
int answer;
final int MIN_NUM = 1;
final int MAX_NUM = 4;
stringAnswer = JOptionPane.showInputDialog(
    "Please enter a number in the range of " + MIN_NUM +
    " to " + MAX_NUM + ": ");
answer = Integer.parseInt(stringAnswer);
while((answer < MIN_NUM || answer > MAX_NUM)
{
    stringAnswer = JOptionPane.showInputDialog(
        "Number must be between " + MIN_NUM + " and " +
        MAX_NUM + ". Please try again: ");
    answer = Integer.parseInt(stringAnswer);
}
```

Exercise 5-9: Validating User Input

In this exercise, you use what you have learned about validating user input to answer Questions 1–3.

1. You plan to use the following statement in a Java program to validate user input:

    ```
    while(inputString.compareTo("") == 0)
    ```

    What would your user enter to cause this test to be **true**?

    _____

2. You plan to use the following statement in a Java program to validate user input:

    ```
    while((userAnswer.compareTo("N") == 0) ||
    (userAnswer.compareTo("n") == 0))
    ```

    What would a user enter to cause this test to be **true**?

    _____

3. You plan to use the following statement in a Java program to validate user input:

    ```
    while(userAnswer < 4 || userAnswer > 10)
    ```

    What would a user enter to cause this test to be true?

    _____

LAB 5.7 Validating User Input

In this lab, you will make additions to a Java program provided with the data files for this book. The program is a guessing game. A random number between 1 and 10 is generated in the program. The user enters a number between 1 and 10, trying to guess the correct number. If the user guesses correctly, the program congratulates the user, and then the loop that controls guessing numbers exits; otherwise the program asks the user if he or she wants to guess again. If the user enters "Y", he or she can guess again. If the user enters "N", the loop exits. You can see that the "Y" or "N" is the sentinel value that controls the loop. Note that the entire program has been written for you. You need to add code that validates correct input, which is "Y" or "N" when the user is asked if he or she wants to guess a number, and a number in the range of 1 through 10 when the user is asked to guess a number.

1. Open the source code file named GuessNumber.java using Notepad or the text editor of your choice.

2. Write loops that validate input at all places in the code where the user is asked to provide input. Comments have been included in the code to help you identify where these loops should be written.

3. Save this source code file in a directory of your choice, and then make that directory your working directory.

4. Compile the source code file GuessNumber.java.

5. Execute the program. See if you can guess the randomly generated number. Execute the program several times to see if the random number changes. Also, test the program to verify that incorrect input is handled correctly. On your best attempt, how many guesses did you have to take to guess the correct number?

Using Arrays in Java Programs

After studying this chapter, you will be able to:

- ◎ Use arrays in Java programs
- ◎ Search an array for a particular value
- ◎ Use parallel arrays in a Java program

You should do the exercises and labs in this chapter after you have finished Chapter 6 of *Programming Logic and Design, Sixth Edition.* In this chapter, you learn how to use Java to declare and initialize arrays. You then access the elements of an array to assign values and process them within your program. You also learn why it is important to stay within the bounds of an array. In addition, you study some programs written in Java that implement the logic and design presented in *Programming Logic and Design, Sixth Edition.*

Array Basics

An **array** is a group of data items in which every item has the same data type, is referenced using the same variable name, and is stored in consecutive memory locations. To reference individual elements in an array, you use a subscript. Think of a **subscript** as the position number of a value within an array. It is important for you to know that in Java, subscript values begin with 0 (zero) and end with *n-1*, where *n* is the number of items stored in the array. You might be tempted to think that the first value in an array would be element number 1, but in fact it would be element number 0. The fifth element in an array would be element number 4.

To use an array in a Java program, you must learn how to declare an array, initialize an array with predetermined values, access array elements, and stay within the bounds of an array. In the next section you'll focus on declaring arrays.

Declaring Arrays

Before you can use an array in a Java program, you must first **declare** it. That is, you must give it a name and specify the data type for the data that will be stored in it. In some cases, you also specify the number of items that will be stored in the array. The following code shows how to declare two arrays, one named `cityPopulations` that will be used to store four `int`s and another named `cities` that will be used to store four `String`s:

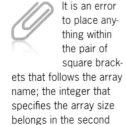

It is an error to place anything within the pair of square brackets that follows the array name; the integer that specifies the array size belongs in the second pair of brackets.

```
int cityPopulations[] = new int[4];
String cities[] = new String[4];
```

As shown, you begin by specifying the data type of the items that will be stored in the array. The data type is followed by the name of the array and then a pair of square brackets.

The `new` operator is used to allocate enough memory for the array elements, based on the data type specified and the integer value placed within the second pair of square brackets that follow the data type.

As shown in Figure 6-1, the compiler allocates enough consecutive memory locations to store four elements of data type `int` for the array named `cityPopulations`. If `cityPopulations[0]` is stored at memory address 1000, then the address of `cityPopulations[1]` is 1004 because each `int` requires 4 bytes of memory. Similarly, `cityPopulations[3]` is at address 1012.

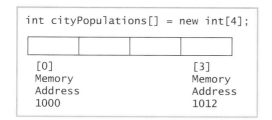

```
int cityPopulations[] = new int[4];
```

[0]   [3]
Memory   Memory
Address   Address
1000   1012

If an array is declared to store items of data type **double**, 8 bytes are allocated for each item in the array.

Figure 6-1   Memory allocation for `cityPopulations` array

The `cityPopulations` array provides an example of how memory is allocated for arrays that contain primitive data types. Memory allocation is different for arrays of objects. Because a `String` is an object in Java, not a primitive data type, memory is allocated for references to a `String` object rather than the `String` object itself. A **reference** is the memory address of an object. The memory for the `String` object is allocated when the `String` object is created. This is shown in Figure 6-2.

```
String cities[] = new String[4];
```

| 1200 | | | | | Chicago |

[0]   [3]   Memory
Memory   Memory   Address
Address   Address   1200
1000   1012

Figure 6-2   Memory allocation for `cities` array

In Figure 6-2, the compiler allocates enough consecutive memory locations to store four references to `String` objects for the array named `cities`. If the address of `cities[0]` is 1000, the address of `cities[1]` is 1004, and the address of `cities[3]` is 1012 because each reference requires 4 bytes of memory. When a `String` object is created, the compiler allocates memory for it at another memory address. This address is then stored in the array. If the first `String` object created stores the name of the city, "Chicago", and the memory allocated for "Chicago" begins at address 1200, then address 1200 is stored in the first element of the array. An example of creating `String` objects is presented later in this chapter.

Initializing Arrays

In Java, array elements are automatically initialized to 0 (zero) for numeric data types and to the value null for references. **Null** is a special value in Java, and it is the zero value for references.

You can and will sometimes want to initialize arrays with values that you choose. This can be done when you declare the array. To initialize an array when you declare it, use curly braces to surround a comma-delimited list of data items, as shown in the following example:

```
int cityPopulations[] = {9500000, 871100, 23900, 40100};
String cities[] = {"Chicago","Detroit","Batavia","Lima"};
```

You can also use assignment statements to provide values for array elements after an array is declared, as in the following example:

```
cityPopulations[0] = 9500000;
cities[0] = "Chicago";
```

A loop is often used to assign values to the elements in an array, as shown here:

```
for(loopIndex = 0; loopIndex < 3; loopIndex++)
{
    cityPopulations[loopIndex] = 12345;
    cities[loopIndex] = "AnyCity";
}
```

The first time this loop is encountered, loopIndex is assigned the value 0. Because 0 is less than 3, the body of the loop executes, assigning the value 12345 to cityPopulations[0] and the value "AnyCity" to cities[0]. Next, the value of loopIndex is incremented and takes on the value 1. Because 1 is less than 3, the loop executes a second time, and the value 12345 is assigned to cityPopulations[1], and "AnyCity" is assigned to cities[1]. Each time the loop executes, the value of loopIndex is incremented. This allows you to access a different location in the arrays each time the body of the loop executes.

Accessing Array Elements

Remember that subscript values begin with 0 (zero) in Java.

You need to access individual locations in an array when you assign a value to an array element, print its value, change its value, assign the value to another variable, and so forth. In Java, you use an integer expression placed in square brackets to indicate which element in the array you want to access. This integer expression is the subscript.

The following Java program declares an array of data type double, initializes an array of data type double, copies values from one array to another, changes several values stored in the array named target, and prints the values of the arrays named source and target.

You can compile and execute this program if you like. It is stored in the file named `ArrayTest.java`.

```java
public class ArrayTest
{
    public static void main(String args[])
    {
        double target[] = new double[3];
        double source[] = {1.0, 5.5, 7.9};
        int loopIndex;
        // Copy values from source to target.
        for(loopIndex = 0; loopIndex < 3; loopIndex++)
            target[loopIndex] = source[loopIndex];
        // Assign values to two elements of target.
        target[0] = 2.0;
        target[1] = 4.5;
        // Print values stored in source and target.
        for(loopIndex = 0; loopIndex < 3; loopIndex++)
        {
            System.out.println("Source " + source[loopIndex]);
            System.out.println("Target " + target[loopIndex]);
        }
    }
}
```

Later in this chapter, you will learn how to use a named constant in an array declaration.

Staying Within the Bounds of an Array

As a Java programmer, you must be careful to ensure that the subscript values you use to access array elements are within the legal bounds. The Java interpreter checks to make sure that a subscript used in your program is greater than or equal to 0 and less than the length of the array. For example, suppose you declare an array named `numbers` as follows:

When using a loop to access array elements, be sure that the test you use to terminate the loop keeps you within the legal bounds, 0 to *n-1*, where *n* is the number of items stored in the array.

```java
int numbers[] = new int[10];
```

In this case, Java checks to make sure the subscripts you use to access this array are integer values between 0 and 9.

If you access an array element that is not in the legal bounds, Java generates an `ArrayIndexOutOfBoundsException`. Generally speaking, an **exception** is an event that disrupts the normal flow of program execution and can cause your program to terminate. You learn about other exceptions that Java throws in other chapters in this book. Here, we concentrate on the `ArrayIndexOutOfBoundsException`.

For example, consider the highlighted operator in the following code, which is taken from the previous Java program example:

```java
double source[] = {1.0, 5.5, 7.9};
int loopIndex;
for(loopIndex = 0; loopIndex < 3; loopIndex++)
```

If you change the highlighted operator to `<=`, as shown here, your program will still compile with no errors:

```
for(loopIndex = 0; loopIndex <= 3; loopIndex++)
```

A problem arises, however, when the Java interpreter executes your program, because the loop will execute when the value of `loopIndex` is 3. When you access the array element, `source[3]`, you are outside the bounds of the array because there is no such element in this array. As shown in Figure 6-3, an `ArrayIndexOutOfBoundsException` is thrown, and your program terminates.

Figure 6-3 `ArrayIndexOutOfBoundsException`

Using Constants with Arrays

It is a good programming practice to use a named constant to help you stay within the bounds of an array when you write programs that declare and access arrays. In Java, you can use a named constant that you create or you can use a constant that Java automatically creates for you to represent the array size.

The following example shows how to use a named constant that you create:

```
final int NUM_ITEMS = 3;
double target[] = new double[NUM_ITEMS];
for(loopIndex = 0; loopIndex < NUM_ITEMS; loopIndex++)
        target[loopIndex] = loopIndex + 10;
```

In Java, after you declare the array named `target`, its size is automatically stored in a field named `target.length`. You can use this value in your Java programs, as shown in the following code sample. In this sample, the field `target.length` is highlighted, so you can spot it easily.

```
final int NUM_ITEMS = 3;
double target[] = new double[NUM_ITEMS];
for(loopIndex = 0; loopIndex < target.length; loopIndex++)
        target[loopIndex] = loopIndex + 10;
```

When you use the Java-created constant, `length`, to represent the size of an array, it is still good practice to use a named constant when declaring an array. That way, if you must alter the code to change the array size, you only have to make the change in one location in your code.

Exercise 6-1: Array Basics

In this exercise, you use what you have learned about declaring and initializing arrays to answer Questions 1–3.

1. Write array declarations for each of the following:

    a. Six book prices

    _____

    b. Three CD titles

    _____

    c. 15 whole numbers

    _____

2. Declare and initialize arrays that store the following:

    a. The ages 22, 34, 7, 62, and 52

    b. The names John, Laila, and Ed

    c. The prices 7.00, 95.00, and 17.50

3. Write an assignment statement that assigns the value 99 to the first element of an array of integers named `miles`.

LAB 6.1 Using Arrays

In this lab, you complete a partially prewritten Java program that uses an array. The program prompts the user to interactively enter 10 integer values, which the program stores in an array. It should then find the minimum and maximum values stored in the array, as well as the average of the 10 values. The data file provided for this lab includes the input statement and some variable declarations. Comments are included in the file to help you write the remainder of the program.

1. Open the source code file named `MinMax.java` using Notepad or the text editor of your choice.

2. Write the Java statements as indicated by the comments.

3. Save this source code file in a directory of your choice, and then make that directory your working directory.

4. Compile the source code file, `MinMax.java`.

5. Execute the program. Enter the following values: 33, 12, –6, 1001, 57, –1, 999, 365, 921, 724. The minimum value should be –6 and the maximum value should be 1001. The average should be 410.5.

Searching an Array for an Exact Match

One of the programs discussed in *Programming Logic and Design,
Sixth Edition* uses an array to hold valid item numbers for a mail-
order business. The idea is that when a customer orders an item,
you can determine if the customer ordered a valid item number by
searching through the array for that item number. This program relies
on a technique called setting a flag to verify that an item exists in an
array. The pseudocode and the Java code for this program are shown
in Figure 6-4.

```
start
    Declarations
        num item
        num SIZE = 6
        num VALID_ITEM[SIZE] = 106, 108, 307,
            405, 457, 688
        num sub
        string foundIt
        num badItemCount = 0
        string MSG_YES = "Item available"
        string MSG_NO = "Item not found"
        num FINISH = 999
    getReady()
    while item <> FINISH
        findItem()
    endwhile
    finishUp()
stop

getReady()
    output "Enter item number or ", FINISH, " to quit"
    input item
return

findItem()
    foundIt = "N"
    sub = 0
    while sub < SIZE
        if item = VALID_ITEM[sub] then
            foundIt = "Y"
        endif
        sub = sub + 1
    endwhile
    if foundIt = "Y" then
        output MSG_YES
    else
        output MSG_NO
```

Figure 6-4 Pseudocode and Java code for the Mail Order program *(continues)*

(continued)

```
        badItemCount = badItemCount + 1
    endif
    output "Enter next item number or ", FINISH, " to quit"
    input item
return

finishUp()
    output badItemCount, " items had invalid numbers"
return
```

```java
import javax.swing.*;
public class MailOrder
{
    public static void main(String args[])
    {
        int item, badItemCount = 0;
        String itemString;
        final int SIZE = 6;
        int VALID_ITEM[] = {106, 108, 307, 405, 457, 688};
        int sub;
        boolean foundIt = false;
        final String MSG_YES = "Item Available";
        final String MSG_NO = "Item not found";
        final int FINISH = 999;

        // This is the work done in the getReady() method
        itemString = JOptionPane.showInputDialog(
                    "Enter item number: ");
        item = Integer.parseInt(itemString);

        while(item != FINISH)
        {
            // This is the work done in the findItem() method
            foundIt = false;
            sub = 0;
            while(sub < SIZE)
            {
                if(item == VALID_ITEM[sub])
                {
                    foundIt = true;
                }
                sub++;
            }
            if(foundIt == true)
            {
                System.out.println(MSG_YES);
            }
```

 The program can be found in the file named MailOrder.java. You may want to compile and execute the program to see how it operates.

Figure 6-4 Pseudocode and Java code for the Mail Order program *(continues)*

(continued)

```
        else
        {
            System.out.println(MSG_NO);
            badItemCount++;
        }
        itemString = JOptionPane.showInputDialog(
                "Enter next item number or " +
                FINISH + " to quit ");
        item = Integer.parseInt(itemString);
    }
    // This is the work done in the finishUp() method
    System.out.println(badItemCount +
                        " items had invalid numbers"
    System.exit(0);
    }
}
```

Figure 6-4 Pseudocode and Java code for the Mail Order program

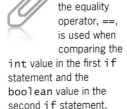 Notice that the equality operator, ==, is used when comparing the int value in the first if statement and the boolean value in the second if statement.

As shown in Figure 6-4, when you translate the pseudocode to Java, you make a few changes. In both the pseudocode and the Java code, the variable named foundIt is the flag. However, in the Java code you assign the value false instead of the string constant "N" to the variable named foundIt. This is because the variable named foundIt is declared as a variable of the boolean type. The boolean data type is one of Java's primitive data types and is only used to store true and false values. Also, notice the pseudocode includes one statement to get the user's item number, whereas it takes two statements in Java to get the user's input.

Exercise 6-2: Searching an Array for an Exact Match

In this exercise, you use what you have learned about searching an array for an exact match. Study the following code, and then answer Questions 1–4. Note that this code may contain errors.

```
String states[] = {"Illinois", "Ohio", "Iowa", "Texas"};
int saveIt, i;
final int MAX_STATES = 4;
String inState;
inState = JOptionPane.showInputDialog("Enter state name:");
for(i = 0; i <= MAX_STATES; i++)
{
    if(inState == states[i])
    {
        saveIt = true;
    }
}
```

1. Is the for loop written correctly?

   _____

   If not, how can you fix it?

   _____

2. Which variable is the flag?

   _____

3. Is the flag variable declared correctly?

   _____

   If not, what should you do to fix it?

   _____

4. Is the comparison in the if statement done correctly?

   _____

   If not, how can you fix it?

   _____

LAB 6.2   Searching an Array for an Exact Match

In this lab, you use what you have learned about searching an array to find an exact match to complete a partially prewritten Java program. The program uses an array that contains valid area codes for 10 cities in the United States. You ask the user of the program to enter an area code; your program then searches the array for that area code. If it is not found, the program should print a message that informs the user that the area code is not found in the list of valid area codes.

The data file provided for this lab includes the input statements and the necessary variable declarations. You need to use a loop to examine all the items in the array and test for a match. You also need to set a flag if there is a match, and then test the flag variable to determine if you should print the "Area code not found" message. Comments in the code tell you where to write your statements. You can use the Mail Order program in this chapter as a guide.

1. Open the source code file named AreaCodes.java using Notepad or the text editor of your choice.

2. Study the prewritten code to make sure you understand it.

3. Write a loop statement that examines the area codes stored in the array.

4. Write code that tests for a match.

5. Write code that, when appropriate, prints the message: "Area code not found."

6. Save this source code file in a directory of your choice, and then make that directory your working directory.

7. Compile the source code file, AreaCodes.java.

8. Execute the program using the following as input:

208
219
253
630

Parallel Arrays

As you learned in *Programming Logic and Design, Sixth Edition*, you use parallel arrays to store values and to maintain a relationship between the items stored in the arrays. Figure 6-5 shows that the student ID number stored in stuID[0] and the grade stored in grades[0] are related—student 56 received a grade of 99.

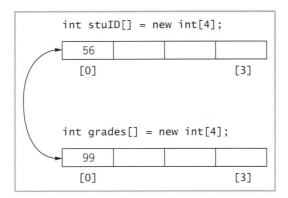

Figure 6-5 Parallel arrays

This relationship is established by using the same subscript value when accessing each array. Note that as the programmer, you must maintain this relationship in your code by always using the same subscript. Java does not create or maintain the relationship.

One of the programs discussed in *Programming Logic and Design, Sixth Edition* is an expanded version of the Mail Order program discussed in the "Searching An Array for an Exact Match" section earlier in this chapter. In the expanded program, you need to determine the price of the ordered item and print the item number along with the price. You use parallel arrays to help you organize the data for the program. One array, VALID_ITEM, contains six valid item numbers. The other array, VALID_PRICE, contains six valid prices. Each price is in the same position as the corresponding item number in the other array. When a customer orders an item, you search the VALID_ITEM array for the customer's item number. When the item number is found, you use the price stored in the same location of the VALID_PRICE array and then output the item number and the price. The complete Java program is stored in the file named MailOrder2.java. The pseudocode and Java code that search the VALID_ITEM array, use a price from the VALID_PRICE array, and then print the ordered item and its price are shown in Figure 6-6.

```
start
    Declarations
        num item
        num price
        num SIZE = 6
        num VALID_ITEM[SIZE] = 106, 108, 307,
            405, 457, 688
        num VALID_PRICE[SIZE] = 0.59, 0.99,
            4.50, 15.99, 17.50, 39.00
        num sub
        string foundIt
        num badItemCount = 0
        string MSG_YES = "Item available"
        string MSG_NO = "Item not found"
        num FINISH = 999
    getReady()
    while item <> FINISH
        findItem()
    endwhile
    finishUp()
stop

getReady()
    output "Enter item number or ", FINISH, " to quit"
    input item
return

findItem()
    foundIt = "N"
    sub = 0
    while sub < SIZE
        if item = VALID_ITEM[sub] then
            foundIt = "Y"
            price = VALID_PRICE[sub]
        endif
        sub = sub + 1
    endwhile
```

Figure 6-6 Pseudocode and Java code for the Mail Order 2 program *(continues)*

(continued)

```
    if foundIt = "Y" then
       output MSG_YES
       output "The price of ", item, " is ", price
    else
       output MSG_NO
       badItemCount = badItemCount + 1
    endif
    output "Enter next item number or ", FINISH, " to quit"
    input item
return

finishUp()
    output badItemCount, " items had invalid numbers"
return
```

```
import javax.swing.*;
public class MailOrder2
{
    public static void main(String args[])
    {
        int item, badItemCount = 0;
        double price;
        String itemString;
        final int SIZE = 6;
        int VALID_ITEM[] = {106, 108, 307, 405, 457, 688};
        double VALID_PRICE[] = {0.59, 0.99, 4.50, 15.99,
                                17.50, 39.00};
        int sub;
        boolean foundIt = false;
        final String MSG_YES = "Item Available";
        final String MSG_NO = "Item not found";
        final int FINISH = 999;

        // This is the work done in the getReady() method
        itemString = JOptionPane.showInputDialog(
                    "Enter next item number or " +
                    FINISH + " to quit ");
        item = Integer.parseInt(itemString);

        while(item != FINISH)
        {
            // This is the work done in the findItem() method
            foundIt = false;
            sub = 0;
            while(sub < SIZE)
            {
                if(item == VALID_ITEM[sub])
```

Figure 6-6 Pseudocode and Java code for the Mail Order 2 program *(continues)*

(continued)

```
                    {
                        foundIt = true;
                        price = VALID_PRICE[sub];
                    }
                    sub++;
                }
                if(foundIt == true)
                {
                    System.out.println(MSG_YES);
                    System.out.println("The price of " + item +
                                    " is " + price);
                }
                else
                {
                    System.out.println(MSG_NO);
                    badItemCount++;
                }
                itemString = JOptionPane.showInputDialog(
                            "Enter next item number or " +
                            FINISH + " to quit ");
                item = Integer.parseInt(itemString);
            }
            // This is the work done in the finishUp() method
            System.out.println(badItemCount +
                            " items had invalid numbers"
            System.exit(0);
        }
    }
```

Figure 6-6   Pseudocode and Java code for the Mail Order 2 program

Exercise 6-3: Parallel Arrays

In this exercise, you use what you have learned about parallel arrays.
Study the following code, and then answer Questions 1–4. Note that
this code may contain errors.

```
String cities[4] = "Batavia", "Gary", "Westmont", "Plano";
int populations[4] = 23900, 102700, 24300, 5700;
final int MAX_CITIES = 4;
int foundIt;
int i, x;
String inCity;
inCity = JOptionPane.showInputDialog("Enter city name: ");
for(i = 0; i = MAX_CITIES; ++i)
{
    if(inCity.compareTo(cities[i]) == 0)
    {
        foundIt = i;
    }
}
System.out.println("Zip code for " + cities[foundIt] +
                    " is " + zipCodes[foundIt]);
```

1. Are the arrays declared and initialized correctly?

   _____

   If not, how can you fix them?

   _____

2. Is the `for` loop written correctly?

   _____

   If not, how can you fix it?

   _____

3. As written, how many times will the `for` loop execute?

   _____

4. How would you describe the purpose of the statement `foundIt = i;`?

   _____

LAB 6.3 Parallel Arrays

In this lab, you use what you have learned about parallel arrays to complete a partially completed Java program. The program is described in Chapter 6, Exercise 6 in *Programming Logic and Design, Sixth Edition*. The program should either print the name and price for a fast-food item from the Billy Goat Fast Food Restaurant or it should print the message: "Sorry, we do not carry that."

Read the problem description carefully before you begin. The data file provided for this lab includes the necessary variable declarations and input statements. You need to write the part of the program that searches for the name of the food item and either prints the name and price of the food item or prints the error message if the item is not found. Comments in the code tell you where to write your statements. You can use the expanded Mail Order 2 program shown in Figure 6-6 as a guide.

1. Open the source code file named `BillyGoat.java` using Notepad or the text editor of your choice.

2. Study the prewritten code to make sure you understand it.

3. Write the code that searches the array for the name of the food item ordered by the customer.

4. Write the code that prints the name and price of the food item or the error message.

5. Save this source code file in a directory of your choice, and then make that directory your working directory.

6. Compile the source code file, `BillyGoat.java`.

7. Execute the program using the following data, and record the output:

   Fries
   Pepsi
   Brat
   Pretzels
   Chips
   Coke
   Cheeseburger
   Hamburger

 Remember that Java is case sensitive, which means it distinguishes between uppercase letters and lowercase letters. This means, for example, that Pepsi is not the same as pepsi.

File Handling and Applications

After studying this chapter, you will be able to:

- ◎ Understand computer files
- ◎ Understand the data hierarchy
- ◎ Perform file operations
- ◎ Work with sequential files and control break logic

In this chapter, you learn how to open and close files in Java, how to use Java to read data from and write data to a file in a program, and how to work with sequential files in a Java program. You should do the exercises and labs in this chapter after you have finished Chapter 7 in *Programming Logic and Design, Sixth Edition*.

File Handling

Business applications are often required to manipulate large amounts of data that is stored in one or more files. As you learned in Chapter 7 of *Programming Logic and Design, Sixth Edition*, data is organized in a hierarchy. At the lowest level of the hierarchy is a **field**, which is a group of characters. On the next level up is a **record**, which is a group of related fields. For example, you could write a program that processes employee records, with each employee record consisting of three fields: the employee's first name, the employee's last name, and the employee's department number.

In Java, to use the data stored in a file, the program must first open the file and then read the data from the file. You use prewritten classes that are part of the Java Standard Edition Development Kit (JDK) to accomplish this. In the next section, you learn how to import packages and classes to make the `BufferedReader` and `FileReader` classes available in your programs. You will also learn how to use these classes to open a file, close a file, read data from a file, and write data to a file.

Importing Packages and Classes

A **package** is a group of related classes. The classes that you need in this chapter are part of a package named `java.io`. The JDK contains many classes that are prewritten for you by the Java development team. You can simplify your programming tasks by creating objects using these classes. You can then use the attributes and methods of those objects in your Java programs.

In order to use these prewritten classes, you must import them into your Java program. You use the `import` keyword to include a class from a Java package. The following code imports the `BufferedReader` class from the Java package named `java.io`.

```
import java.io.BufferedReader;
```

You can also use the * (asterisk) character in an import statement to import all classes from a package rather than specifying a single class. The following code imports all of the classes in the `java.io` package.

The Java programs in this chapter will use this style to import the classes needed to perform file input and output.

```
import java.io.*;
```

The import statement tells the Java compiler the name of the package and the name of the class (or classes) that contains the prewritten code you want to use. The Java compiler will automatically include this code.

Opening a File for Reading

To open a file and read data into a Java program, you instantiate a FileReader object and specify the name of the file to associate with the object. Look at the following example:

```
FileReader fr = new FileReader("inputFile.txt");
```

In the example, the new keyword instantiates a FileReader object. This new object is associated with the file named inputFile.txt. Notice that the name of the file is enclosed in double quotes and placed within parentheses. As a result of the assignment statement, this newly created FileReader object is assigned to a variable named fr and may now be referred to in your Java program using the name fr. In addition, the statement opens the file named inputFile.txt for reading. This means that the program can now read data from the file. In this example, the file named inputFile.txt must be saved in the same folder as the Java program that is using the file. To open a file that is saved in a different folder, a path must be specified as in the next example.

```
FileReader fr = new FileReader(
    "C:\myJavaPrograms\Chapter7\inputFile.txt");
```

Even though the program can now read from the file, it is usually more efficient to read from a buffered file. To do this, we need to create a BufferedReader object. A FileReader object reads data from a file one character at a time, whereas a BufferedReader object can read data a line at a time. In order to create a BufferedReader object, we decorate the FileReader object. **Decorating** is a way of adding functionality to objects in Java. Here is an example:

```
BufferedReader br = new BufferedReader(fr);
```

In this example, a new BufferedReader object is created by adding functionality to the FileReader object named fr. The name of the BufferedReader variable is br. You will use the name br to refer to the BufferedReader object in your Java program.

Reading Data from an Input File

Once you have created a new `BufferedReader` object that decorates a `FileReader` object, you are ready to read the data in the file. The `BufferedReader` class provides this functionality with the `readLine()` method. The `readLine()` method allows the program to read a line from an input file. A **line** is defined as all of the characters up to a **newline** character or up to the **End Of File (EOF)** marker. The newline character is generated when you press the Enter key on the keyboard. The EOF marker is automatically placed at the end of a file when it is saved.

We will assume that the input file for a program is organized so that an employee's first name is on one line, followed by his last name on the next line, followed by his salary on the third, as follows:

Tim
Moriarty
4000.00

To allow the program to read this data, you would write the following Java code:

```
String firstName, lastName, salaryString;
double salary;
firstName = br.readLine();
lastName = br.readLine();
salaryString = br.readLine();
```

Because the `readLine()` method always returns a `String`, the first line in the example declares three `String` variables named `firstName`, `lastName`, and `salaryString`. The next line declares a `double` named `salary`. Next, the `readLine()` method is used three times to read the three lines of input from the file associated with the `BufferedReader` object named `br`. After this code executes, the variable named `firstName` contains the value "Tim", the variable named `lastName` contains the value "Moriarty", and the variable named `salaryString` contains the value 4000.00. As you have previously learned, if your program requires the use of an employee's salary in a numeric calculation, you must convert `salaryString` to a `double` as follows:

```
salary = Double.parseDouble(salaryString);
```

The next example illustrates how to read a salary and convert it to a `double` in one step. This technique allows you to omit declaring the `salaryString` variable.

```
salary = Double.parseDouble(br.readLine());
```

Reading Data Using a Loop and EOF

In a program that has to read large amounts of data, it is usually best to have the program use a loop. In the loop, the program continues to read from the file until EOF (end of file) is encountered. The readLine() method returns a null value when EOF is reached. The Java code that follows shows how to use the readLine() method as part of a loop.

```
while((firstName = br.readLine()) != null)
{
      // body of loop
}
```

In this example, the readLine() method is part of the expression to be tested. As long as the value returned by readLine() is not equal to null, the expression is true, and the loop is entered. As soon as EOF is encountered, the test becomes false, and the program exits the loop. The parentheses are used to control precedence.

Opening a File for Writing

To write data from a Java program to an output file, the program must first open a file. This is a two-step process: first, the program must instantiate a FileWriter object and then specify the name of the file to associate with the object. Look at the following example:

```
FileWriter fw = new FileWriter("outputFile.txt");
```

In this example, the new keyword is used to instantiate a FileWriter object. This object is associated with the file named outputFile.txt. Notice that the name of the file is enclosed in double quotes and placed within parentheses. As a result of the assignment statement, this newly created FileWriter object is assigned to a variable named fw. You can now refer to the object in your Java program using the name fw. In addition, the statement opens the file named outputFile.txt for writing. This means that the program can now write data to the file.

As with input files, it's a good idea to decorate the FileWriter object to add functionality. For example, you can add the functionality that is included in the PrintWriter class, which provides the ability to flush (that is, empty) and close an output file. In Java, a write operation is not complete until the buffer associated with an output file is **flushed** (emptied) and **closed** (made unavailable for further output). The following example shows how to decorate the FileWriter object by adding functionality from the PrintWriter class.

```
PrintWriter pw = new PrintWriter(fw);
```

In this example, a new `PrintWriter` object is created by adding functionality to the `FileWriter` object named fw. The name of the `PrintWriter` object is pw. From this point on, we can use the name pw to refer to the `PrintWriter` object in our Java program.

Writing Data to an Output File

Once you have decorated a `FileWriter` object with a `PrintWriter` object, the program is ready to write data to a file. You can use the `println()` method (which is included in the `PrintWriter` class) to write a line to an output file.

As an example, assume that an employee's `firstName`, `lastName`, and `salary` have been read from an input file as in the previous example and that the employee is to receive a 15 percent salary increase that is calculated as follows:

```
final double INCREASE = 1.15;
double newSalary;
newSalary = salary * INCREASE;
```

You now want to write the employee's `firstName`, `lastName`, and newSalary to the output file name newSalary2011.txt. The code that follows accomplishes this task.

```
FileWriter fw = new FileWriter("newSalary2011.txt");
PrintWriter pw = new PrintWriter(fw);
pw.println(firstName);
pw.println(lastName);
pw.println(newSalary);
pw.flush();
pw.close();
```

The Java program shown in Figure 7-1 implements the file input and output operations discussed in this section.

```
// EmployeeRaise.java - This program reads employee first
// and last names and salaries from an input file,
// calculates a 15% raise, and writes the employee's first
// and last name and new salary to an output file.
// Input:  employees.txt.
// Output: newSalary2011.txt

import java.io.*;  // Import class for file input.
```

Figure 7-1 Reading and writing file data *(continues)*

(continued)

```java
public class EmployeeRaise
{
    public static void main(String args[]) throws Exception
    {
        String firstName, lastName, salaryString;
        double salary, newSalary;
        final double INCREASE = 1.15;

        // Open input file.
        FileReader fr = new FileReader("employees.txt");
        // Create BufferedReader object.
        BufferedReader br = new BufferedReader(fr);

        // Open output file.
        FileWriter fw = new FileWriter("newSalary2011.txt");
        PrintWriter pw = new PrintWriter(fw);

        // Read records from file and test for EOF.
        while((firstName = br.readLine()) != null)
        {
            lastName = br.readLine();
            salaryString = br.readLine();
            salary = Double.parseDouble(salaryString);
            newSalary = salary * INCREASE;
            pw.println(lastName);
            pw.println(firstName);
            pw.println(newSalary);
            pw.flush();
        }

        br.close();
        pw.close();
        System.exit(0);
    } // End of main() method.
} // End of EmployeeRaise class.
```

Figure 7-1   Reading and writing file data

When writing code that opens files and writes to files, you need to be aware of potential problems. For example, the program might try to open a nonexistent file or it might try to read beyond the EOF marker. If these events occur, a Java program will generate an exception. (An **exception** is an event that occurs that disrupts the normal flow of execution.) The Java compiler knows that certain methods are capable of causing an exception. If these methods are used in a program, it will fail to compile unless you include the words throws Exception as part of the header for the main() method, as shown in Figure 7-1. By including these words, you are telling the Java compiler that you know an exception could occur, and the compiler should assume that the program contains code that will handle the exception, should it occur. A section of code that is designed to solve problems related to exceptions is known as an **exception handler.**

There is much more to learn about the input and output classes in the `java.io` package, but you will be able to accomplish quite a lot using what you have learned in this section.

You need to know quite a bit about Java in order to write exception handlers. In this book, we will simply include `throws Exception` in headers to ensure that our programs compile.

Exercise 7-1: Opening Files and Performing File Input

In this exercise, you use what you have learned about opening a file and getting input into a program from a file. Study the following code, and then answer Questions 1–3.

```
1   FileReader fr = new FileReader(myDVDFile.dat);
2   BufferedReader br = new BufferedReader();
3   String dvdName, dvdPrice, dvdShelf;
4   dvdName = br.readLine();
5   dvdPrice = br.readLine();
6   dvdShelf = br.readLine();
```

Figure 7-2   Code for Exercise 7-1

1. Describe the error on line 1, and explain how to fix it.

    _____

2. Describe the error on line 2, and explain how to fix it.

    _____

3. Consider the following data from the input file myDVDFile.dat:

    Lost 35.00 1A
    Watchmen 29.00 2C
    Heroes 39.00 3B

    a. What value is stored in the variable named dvdName?

        _____

    b. What value is stored in the variable name dvdPrice?

        _____

    c. What value is stored in the variable named dvdShelf?

        _____

    d. If there is a problem with the values of these variables, what is the problem and how could you fix it?

        _____

LAB 7.1   Using an Input File

In this lab, you will open a file and read input from that file in a prewritten Java program. The program should read and print the names of fish that are stored in the input file named fish.dat.

1. Open the source code file named Fish.java using Notepad or the text editor of your choice.

2. Declare the variables you will need.

3. Write the Java statements that will open the input file, fish.dat, for reading.

4. Write a while loop to read the input until EOF is reached.

5. In the body of the loop, print the name of each fish.

6. Save this source code file in a directory of your choice, and then make that directory your working directory.

7. Compile the source code file Fish.java.

8. Execute the program.

Understanding Sequential Files and Control Break Logic

As you learned in Chapter 7 of *Programming Logic and Design, Sixth Edition*, a **sequential file** is a file in which records are stored one after another in some order. The records in a sequential file are organized based on the contents of one or more fields, such as ID numbers, part numbers, or last names.

A **single-level control break** program reads data from a sequential file and causes a break in the logic based on the value of a single variable. In Chapter 7 of *Programming Logic and Design, Sixth Edition*, you learned about techniques you can employ to implement a single-level control break program. Be sure you understand these techniques before you continue on with this chapter. The program described in Chapter 7 of *Programming Logic and Design, Sixth Edition* that produces a report of customers by state is an example of a single-level control break program. This program reads a record for each client, keeps a count of the number of clients in each state, and prints a report. As shown in Figure 7-3, the report generated by this program includes clients' names, cities, and states, along with a count of the number of clients in each state.

```
Company Clients by State of Residence

Name                    City                    State

Albertson               Birmingham              Alabama
Davis                   Birmingham              Alabama
Lawrence                Montgomery              Alabama
                                                Count for Alabama      3

Smith                   Anchorage               Alaska
Young                   Anchorage               Alaska
Davis                   Fairbanks               Alaska
Mitchell                Juneau                  Alaska
Zimmer                  Juneau                  Alaska
                                                Count for Alaska       5

Edwards                 Phoenix                 Arizona
                                                Count for Arizona      1
```

Figure 7-3   Control break report with totals after each state

Each client record is made up of the following fields: Name, City, and State. Note the following example records, each made up of three lines:

Albertson
Birmingham
Alabama
Lawrence
Montgomery
Alabama
Smith
Anchorage
Alaska

Remember that input records for a control break program are usually stored in a data file on a storage device, such as a disk, and the records are sorted according to a predetermined control break variable. For example, the control break variable for this program is state, so the input records would be sorted according to state.

Figure 7-4 includes the pseudocode for the Client By State program, and Figure 7-5 shows the Java code that implements the program.

```
Start
   Declarations
      InputFile inFile
      string TITLE = "Company Clients by State of Residence"
      string COL_HEADS = "Name    City    State"
      string name
      string city
      string state
      num count = 0
      String oldState
   getReady()
   while not eof
      produceReport()
   endwhile
   finishUp()
stop

getReady()
   output TITLE
   output COL_HEADS
   open inFile "ClientsByState.dat"
   input name, city, state from inFile
   oldState = state
return
produceReport()
   if state <> oldState then
      controlBreak()
   endif
   output name, city, state
   count = count + 1
   input name, city, state from inFile
return

controlBreak()
   output "Count for ", oldState, count
   count = 0
   oldState = state
return

finishUp()
   output "Count for ", oldState, count
   close inFile
return
```

Figure 7-4   Client By State program pseudocode

```
1  // ClientByState.java - This program creates a report that
2  // lists clients with a count of the number of clients for
3  // each state.
4  // Input:  client.dat
5  // Output:  Report
6
7  import java.io.*;
8
9  public class ClientByState
10 {
11     public static void main(String args[]) throws Exception
12     {
13         // Declarations
14         FileReader fr = new FileReader("client.dat");
15         BufferedReader br = new BufferedReader(fr);
16         final String TITLE =
17                 "\n\nCompany Clients by State of Residence\n\n";
18         String name = "", city = "", state = "";
19         int count = 0;
20         String oldState = "";
21         boolean done;
22
23         // Work done in the getReady() method
24         System.out.println(TITLE);
25         if((name = br.readLine()) != null)
26         {
27             city = br.readLine();
28             state = br.readLine();
29             done = false;
30             oldState = state;
31         }
32         else
33             done = true;
34         while(done == false)
35         {
36             // Work done in the produceReport() method
37             if(state.compareTo(oldState) != 0)
38             {
39                 // Work done in the controlBreak() method
40                 System.out.println("\t\t\tCount for " +
41                                   oldState + " " + count);
42                 count = 0;
43                 oldState = state;
44             }
45             System.out.println(name + " " + city + " " +
46                               state);
47             count++;
```

Figure 7-5   Client By State program written in Java (continues)

(continued)

```
48              if((name = br.readLine()) != null)
49              {
50                  city = br.readLine();
51                  state = br.readLine();
52                  done = false;
53              }
54              else
55                  done = true;
56          }
57          // Work done in the finishUp() method
58          System.out.println("\t\t\tCount for " +
59                              oldState + " " + count);
60          br.close();
61          System.exit(0);
62
63      } // End of main() method.
64  } // End of ClientByState class
```

Figure 7-5   Client By State program written in Java

As you can see in Figure 7-5, the Java program begins on line 1 with comments that describe what the program does. (The line numbers shown in this program are not part of the Java code. They are included for reference only.) The program also includes comments that describe the program's input and output. Next comes the Java code that defines the `ClientByState` class (line 9) and, within the class, the `main()` method (line 11).

Within the `main()` method, lines 14 through 21 declare variables and constants and initialize them when appropriate. Lines 14 and 15 declare variables as well as open the input file named `client.dat`. Lines 24 through 33 include the work done in the `getReady()` method, which includes printing the heading for the report this program generates and performing a priming read. You learned about performing a priming read in Chapter 3 of this book and in Chapter 3 of *Programming Logic and Design, Sixth Edition*.

Notice that the Java code in the priming read (lines 25 through 28) is a little different than the pseudocode. An `if` statement is used on line 25 to test if a client's name was read from the input file or if EOF was encountered. If EOF is not encountered, the result of this test will be `true`, causing the execution of the input statements that read the `city` and `state` from the input file. The `boolean` value `false` is also assigned to the variable named `done` on line 29 followed by assigning the current value of `state` to the variable named `oldState` on line 30. Remember that the variable `state` serves as the control break variable. If EOF is encountered, the result of this test will be `false`, causing the `boolean` value `true` to be assigned to the variable named done on line 33. The `boolean` variable named done is used later in the program to control the `while` loop.

Next comes the `while` loop (line 34), which continues to execute as long as the value of the `boolean` variable done is `false`. The body of the `while` loop contains the work done in the `produceReport()` method. First, an `if` statement uses the `compareTo()` method to test the control break variable `state` on line 37. The `compareTo()` method's job is to determine if the record the program is currently working with has the same state as the previous record's state. If it does not, this indicates the beginning of a new state. As a result, the program performs the work done in the `controlBreak()` method (lines 40 through 43). The work of the `controlBreak()` method does the following:

1. Prints the value of the variable named count that contains the count of clients in the current state (lines 40 and 41).

2. Assigns the value 0 to the variable named count to prepare for the next state.

3. Assigns the value of the variable named `state` to the variable named `oldState` to prepare for the next state.

If the record the program is currently working with has the same state as the previous record's state, the `controlBreak()` method's work is not performed. Whether or not the current record's state is the same state as the previous record's state, the next statement to execute (lines 45 and 46) prints the client's name, city, and state. Then the variable named count is incremented on line 47 followed by the program reading the next client's record on lines 48 through 55 using the same technique as the priming read.

The condition in the `while` loop on line 34 is then tested again, causing the loop to continue executing until the value of the variable named done is `true`. The variable named done is assigned the value `true` when the program encounters EOF when reading from the input file on line 55.

When the `while` loop is exited, the last section of the program executes. This consists of the work done in the `finishUp()` method:

• Printing the value of the variable named count (which is the count of the clients in the last state in the input file) on lines 58 and 59.

• Closing the input file (line 60).

Exercise 7-2: Accumulating Totals in Single-Level Control Break Programs

In this exercise, you will use what you have learned about accumulating totals in a single-level control break program. Study the following code, and then answer Questions 1–4.

```
if(partNum != oldPartNum)
{
    System.out.println("Part Number " + oldPartNum);
    totalParts = partNum;
    oldPartNum = partNum;
}
```

1. What is the control break variable?

   _____

2. True or False? The value of the control break variable should never be changed.

   _____

3. Is `totalParts` being calculated correctly?

   _____

   If not, how can you fix the code?

   _____

4. True or False? In a control break program, it doesn't matter if the records in the input file are in a specified order.

   _____

LAB 7.2 Accumulating Totals in Single-Level Control Break Programs

In this lab, you will use what you have learned about accumulating totals in a single-level control break program to complete a Java program. The program should produce a report for a fast food restaurant owner to help her keep track of the hours worked by her part-time employees. The report should include the day of the week, the number of hours worked by each employee for each day, and the total hours worked by all employees each day. The report should look similar to the one shown in Figure 7-6.

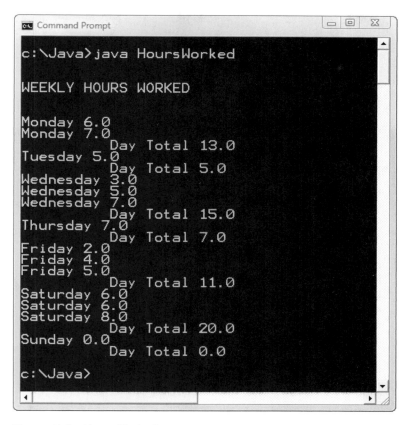

```
c:\Java>java HoursWorked

WEEKLY HOURS WORKED

Monday 6.0
Monday 7.0
          Day Total 13.0
Tuesday 5.0
          Day Total 5.0
Wednesday 3.0
Wednesday 5.0
Wednesday 7.0
          Day Total 15.0
Thursday 7.0
          Day Total 7.0
Friday 2.0
Friday 4.0
Friday 5.0
          Day Total 11.0
Saturday 6.0
Saturday 6.0
Saturday 8.0
          Day Total 20.0
Sunday 0.0
          Day Total 0.0

c:\Java>
```

Figure 7-6 Hours Worked program report

The student file provided for this lab includes the necessary variable declarations and input and output statements. You need to implement the code that recognizes when a control break should occur. You also need to complete the control break code. Be sure to accumulate the daily totals for all days in the week. Comments in the code tell you where to write your code. You can use the Client By State program in this chapter as a guide for this new program.

1. Open the source code file named HoursWorked.java using Notepad or the text editor of your choice.

2. Study the prewritten code to understand what has already been done.

3. Write the control break code, including the code for the dayChange() method, in the main() method.

4. Save this source code file in a directory of your choice, and then make that directory your working directory.

5. Compile the source code file, `HoursWorked.java`.

6. Execute this program using the following input values:

Monday – 6 hours (employee 1), 7 hours (employee 2)
Tuesday – 5 hours (employee 1)
Wednesday – 3 hours (employee 1), 5 hours (employee 2),
7 hours (employee 3)
Thursday – 7 hours (employee 1)
Friday – 2 hours (employee 1), 4 hours (employee 2), 5 hours
(employee 3)
Saturday – 6 hours (employee 1), 6 hours (employee 2),
8 hours (employee 3)
Sunday – 0 hours

The program results should include:

A total of 13 hours worked on Monday
A total of 5 hours worked on Tuesday
A total of 15 hours worked on Wednesday
A total of 7 hours worked on Thursday
A total of 11 hours worked on Friday
A total of 20 hours worked on Saturday
A total of 0 hours worked on Sunday

CHAPTER 8

Advanced Array Techniques

After studying this chapter, you will be able to:

◎ Explain the need to sort data

◎ Swap data values in a program

◎ Create a bubble sort in Java

◎ Work with multidimensional arrays

In this chapter, you review why you might want to sort data, how to use Java to swap two data values in a program, how to create a bubble sort in a Java program, and how to use multidimensional arrays. You should do the exercises and labs in this chapter after you have finished Chapter 8 in *Programming Logic and Design, Sixth Edition*.

Sorting Data

Data records are always stored in some order, but possibly not in the order in which you want to process or view them in your program. When this is the case, you need to give your program the ability to arrange (sort) records in a useful order. For example, the inventory records you need to process might be stored in product number order, but you might need to produce a report that lists products from lowest cost to highest cost. That means your program needs to be able to sort the records by cost.

Sorting makes searching for records easier and more efficient. A human can usually find what she is searching for by simply glancing through a group of data items, but a program must look through a group of data items one by one, making a decision about each one. When searching unsorted records for a particular data value, a program must examine every single record until it either locates the data value or determines that it does not exist. However, when searching sorted records, the program can quickly determine when to stop searching, as shown in the following step-by-step scenario:

1. The records used by your program are sorted by product number.

2. The user is searching for the product number 12367.

3. The program locates the record for product number 12368 but has not yet found product number 12367.

4. The program determines that the record for product number 12367 does not exist and, therefore, stops searching through the list.

Many search algorithms require that data be sorted before it can be searched. (An **algorithm** is a plan for solving a problem.) You can choose from many algorithms for sorting and searching for data. In *Programming Logic and Design, Sixth Edition*, you learned how to swap data values in an array, and you also learned about the bubble sort. Both of these topics are covered in this book.

Swapping Data Values

When you swap values, you place the value stored in one variable into a second variable, and then you place the value that was originally stored in the second variable in the first variable. You must also create a third variable to temporarily hold one of the values you want to swap so that a value is not lost. For example, if you try to swap values using the following code, you will lose the value of score2.

```
int score1 = 90;
int score2 = 85;
score2 = score1; // The value of score2 is now 90.
score1 = score2; // The value of score1 is also 90.
```

However, if you use a variable to temporarily hold one of the values, the swap is successful. This is shown in the following code.

```
int score1 = 90;
int score2 = 85;
int temp;
temp = score2;   // The value of temp is 85.
score2 = score1; // The value of score2 is 90.
score1 = temp;   // The value of score1 is 85.
```

Exercise 8-1: Swapping Values

In this exercise, you use what you have learned about swapping values to answer the following question.

1. Suppose you have declared and initialized two String variables, name1 and name2, in a Java program. Now, you want to swap the values stored in name1 and name2, but only if the value of name1 is greater than the value of name2. Remember that you do not use the equality operator (==) when comparing String objects.

    Write the Java code that accomplishes this task. The declarations are as follows:

    ```
    String name1 = "Smith";
    String name2 = "Smythe";
    ```

    _____

    _____

    _____

    _____

138

LAB 8.1 Swapping Values

In this lab, you will complete a Java program that swaps values stored in three `int` variables and determines maximum and minimum values. The Java file provided for this lab contains the necessary variable declarations, as well as the input and output statements. You want to end up with the smallest value stored in the variable named `value1` and the largest value stored in the variable named `value3`. You need to write the statements that compare the values and swap them if appropriate. Comments included in the code tell you where to write your statements.

1. Open the source code file named `Swap.java` using the text editor of your choice.

2. Write the statements that test the first two integers, and swap them if necessary.

3. Write the statements that test the second and third integer, and swap them if necessary.

4. Write the statements that test the first and second integers again, and swap them if necessary.

5. Save this source code file in a directory of your choice, and then make that directory your working directory.

6. Compile the source code file, `Swap.java`.

7. Execute the program using the following sets of input values, and record the output.

    255 313 –10

    610 993 37

    33 55 33

Using a Bubble Sort

A bubble sort is one of the easiest sorting techniques to understand. However, while it is logically simple, it is not very efficient. If the list contains *n* values, the bubble sort will make *n* – 1 passes over the list. For example, if the list contains 100 values, the bubble sort will make 99 passes over the data. During each pass, it examines successive overlapped pairs and swaps or exchanges those values that are out of order. After one pass over the data, the heaviest (largest) value sinks to the bottom and is then in the correct position in the list.

In *Programming Logic and Design, Sixth Edition*, you learned several ways to refine the bubble sort. One way is to reduce unnecessary comparisons by ignoring the last value in the list in the second pass through the data, because you can be sure it is already positioned correctly. On the third pass, you can ignore the last two values in the list because you know they are already positioned correctly. Thus, in each pass, you can reduce the number of items to be compared, and possibly swapped, by one.

Another refinement to the bubble sort is to eliminate unnecessary passes over the data in the list. When items in the array to be sorted are not entirely out of order, it may not be necessary to make $n - 1$ passes over the data because after several passes, the items may already be in order. You can add a flag variable to the bubble sort, and then test the value of that flag variable to determine whether any swaps have been made in any single pass over the data. If no swaps have been made, you know that the list is in order; therefore, you do not need to continue with additional passes.

You also learned about using a constant for the size of the array to make your logic easier to understand and your programs easier to change and maintain. Finally, you learned how to sort a list of varying size by counting the number of items placed in the array as you read in items.

All of these refinements are included in the pseudocode for the Score Sorting program in Figure 8-1. The Java code that implements the Score Sorting logic is provided in Figure 8-2. The line numbers shown in Figure 8-2 are not part of the Java code. They are provided for reference only.

```
start
    num SIZE = 100
    num score[SIZE]
    num x
    num y
    num temp
    num numberOfEls = 0
    num comparisons
    num QUIT = 999
    String didSwap
    fillArray()
    sortArray()
    displayArray()
stop
```

Figure 8-1 Pseudocode for Score Sorting program *(continues)*

(continued)

```
num fillArray()
   x = 0
   output "Enter a score or ", QUIT, " to quit "
   input score[x]
   x = x + 1
   while x < SIZE AND score[x] <> QUIT
      output "Enter a score or ", QUIT, " to quit "
      input score[x]
      x = x + 1
   endwhile
   numberOfEls = x
   comparisons = numberOfEls - 1
return

void sortArray()
   x = 0
   didSwap = "Yes"
   while didSwap = "Yes"
      x = 0
      didSwap = "No"
      while x < comparisons
         if score[x] > score[x + 1] then
            swap()
            didSwap = "Yes"
         endif
         x = x + 1
      endwhile
      comparisons = comparisons - 1
   endwhile
return

void swap()
   temp = score[x + 1]
   score[x + 1] = score[x]
   score[x] = temp
return

void displayArray()
   x = 0
   while x < numberOfEls
      output score[x]
      x = x + 1
   endwhile
return
```

Figure 8-1 Pseudocode for Score Sorting program

```
 1 // StudentScores.java - This program interactively reads a
 2 // variable number of student test scores, stores the
 3 // scores in an array, and then sorts the scores in
 4 // ascending order.
 5 // Input:  Interactive
 6 // Output:  Sorted list of student scores.
 7
 8 import javax.swing.*;
 9
10 public class StudentScores
11 {
12    public static void main(String args[]) throws Exception
13    {
14       // Declare variables.
15       // Maximum size of array
16       final int SIZE = 100;
17       String stuScoreString;
18       // Array of student scores
19       int score[] = new int[SIZE];
20       int x;
21       int temp;
22       // Actual number of elements in array.
23       int numberOfEls = 0;
24       int comparisons;
25       final int QUIT = 999;
26       Boolean didSwap;
27
28       // Work done in the fillArray() method
29       x = 0;
30       stuScoreString = JOptionPane.showInputDialog(
31             "Enter a score or " + QUIT + " to quit ");
32       score[x] = Integer.parseInt(stuScoreString);
33       x++;
34       while(x < SIZE && score[x - 1] != QUIT)
35       {
36          stuScoreString = JOptionPane.showInputDialog(
37                "Enter a score or " + QUIT + " to quit ");
38          score[x] = Integer.parseInt(stuScoreString);
39          x++;
40       } // End of input loop.
41       numberOfEls = x - 1;
42       comparisons = numberOfEls - 1;
43
44       // Work done in the sortArray() method
45       didSwap = true;// Set flag to true.
46       // Outer loop controls number of passes over data.
47       while(didSwap == true) // Test flag.
48       {
49          x = 0;
50          didSwap = false;
```

Figure 8-2 Java code for Score Sorting program *(continues)*

(continued)

```
51          // Inner loop controls number of items to compare.
52          while(x < comparisons)
53          {
54              if(score[x] > score[x + 1]) // Swap?
55              {
56                  // Work done in the swap() method
57                  temp = score[x + 1];
58                  score[x+1] = score[x];
59                  score[x] = temp;
60                  didSwap = true;
61              }
62              x++;    // Get ready for next pair.
63          }
64          comparisons--;
65      }
66
67      // Work done in the displayArray() method
68      x = 0;
69      while(x < numberOfEls)
70      {
71          System.out.println(score[x]);
72          x++;
73      }
74      System.exit(0);
75   } // End of main() method.
76 } // End of StudentScores class.
```

Figure 8-2   Java code for Score Sorting program

The `main()` Method

As shown in Figure 8-2, the `main()` method (line 12) declares variables and performs the work of the program. The variables include:

- A constant named `SIZE`, initialized with the value 100, which represents the maximum number of items this program can sort

- A `String` variable named `stuScoreString` that is used to hold the `String` version of a student score

- An array of data type `int` named `score` that is used to store up to a maximum of `SIZE` (100) items to be sorted

- An `int` variable named `x` that is used as the array subscript

- An `int` variable named `temp` that is used to swap the values stored in the array

- An `int` named `numberOfEls` that is used to hold the actual number of items stored in the array

- An `int` named `comparisons` that is used to control the number of comparisons that should be done

- An `int` constant named `QUIT`, initialized to 999, that is used to control the `while` loop

- A `Boolean` named `didSwap` that is used as a flag to indicate when a swap has taken place

After these variables are declared, the work done in the `fillArray()` method begins on line 28. The `fillArray()` work is responsible for filling up the array with items to be sorted. On line 44, the work done in the `sortArray()` method begins. This work is responsible for sorting the items stored in the `score` array. Lastly, the work done in the `diplayArray()` method begins on line 67 and is responsible for displaying the sorted scores on the user's screen.

The `fillArray()` Method

The work done in the `fillArray()` method, which begins on line 28 in Figure 8-2, is responsible for: 1) storing the data in the array and 2) counting the actual number of elements placed in the array. The `fillArray()` method assigns the value 0 to the variable named `x` and then performs a priming read (lines 30 and 31) to retrieve the first student score from the user and stores the score in the `String` variable named `stuScoreString`. The `String` version of a student's score, `stuScoreString`, is then converted to an `int` and stored in the array named `score` at location `x` on line 32. Notice that the array subscript variable `x` is initialized to 0 on line 29 because the first position in an array is position 0. Also, notice the variable named `x` is incremented on line 33 because it is used to count the number of scores entered by the user of the program.

On line 34, the condition that controls the `while` loop is tested. The `while` loop executes as long as the number of scores input by the user (represented by the variable named `x`) is less than `SIZE` (100) and as long as the user has not entered 999 (the value of the constant `QUIT`) for the student score. If `x` is less than `SIZE` and the user does not want to quit, there is enough room in the array to store the student score. In that case, the program retrieves the next student score, stores the score in the `String` variable named `stuScoreString`, converts the `String` to an `int`, and then stores the score in the array named `score` at location `x` on line 38. The program then increments the value of `x` (line 39) to get ready to store the next student score in the array. The loop continues to execute until the user enters the value 999 or until there is no more room in the array.

When the program exits the loop, the value of x − 1 is assigned to the variable named `numberOfEls` on line 41. Notice that x is used as the array subscript and that its value is incremented every time the `while` loop executes, including when the user enters the value 999 in order to quit; therefore, x represents the number of student scores the user entered *plus one*. On line 42 the value of `numberOfEls` − 1 is assigned to the variable named `comparisons` and represents the maximum number of elements the bubble sort will compare on a pass over the data stored in the array. It ensures that the program does not attempt to compare item x with item x + 1, when x is the last item in the array.

The `sortArray()` Method

The work done in the `sortArray()` method begins on line 44 and uses a refined bubble sort to rearrange the student scores in the array named `score` to be in ascending order. Refer to Figure 8-1, which includes the pseudocode, and Figure 8-2, which includes the Java code that implements the `sortArray()` method.

Line 45 initializes the flag variable `didSwap` to `true`, because, at this point in the program, it is assumed that items will need to be swapped.

The outer loop (line 47), `while(didSwap == true)`, controls the number of passes over the data. This logic implements one of the refinements discussed earlier—eliminating unnecessary passes over the data. As long as `didSwap` is `true`, the program knows that swaps have been made and that, therefore, the data is still out of order. Thus, when `didSwap` is `true`, the program enters the loop. The first statement in the body of the loop (line 49) is x = 0;. The program assigns the value 0 to x because x is used as the array subscript. Recall that in Java, the first subscript in an array is number 0.

Next, to prepare for comparing the elements in the array, line 50 assigns the value `false` to `didSwap`. This is necessary because the program has not yet swapped any values in the array on this pass. The inner loop begins on line 52. The test, x < `comparisons`, controls the number of pairs of values in the array the program compares on one pass over the data. This implements another of the refinements discussed earlier—reducing unnecessary comparisons. The last statement in the outer loop on line 64, `comparisons--;`, decrements the value of `comparisons` by 1 each time the outer loop executes. The program decrements `comparisons` because, when a complete pass is made over the data, it knows an item is positioned in the array correctly. Comparing the value of `comparisons` with the value of x in the inner loop reduces the number of necessary comparisons made when this loop executes.

On line 54, within the inner loop, adjacent items in the array are accessed and compared using the subscript variable x and x + 1. The adjacent array items are compared to see if the program should swap them. If the values should be swapped, the program executes the statements that make up the work done in the swap() method on lines 57 through 59, which uses the technique discussed earlier to rearrange the two values in the array. Next, line 60 assigns true to the variable named didSwap. The last task performed by the inner loop (line 62) is adding 1 to the value of the subscript variable x. This ensures that the next time through the inner loop, the program will compare the next two adjacent items in the array. The program continues to compare two adjacent items and possibly swap them as long as the value of x is less than the value of comparisons.

The displayArray() Method

In the displayArray() method, you print the sorted array on the user's screen. Figure 8-1 shows the pseudocode for this method. The Java code is shown in Figure 8-2.

The work done in the displayArray() method begins on line 67 of Figure 8-2. Line 68 assigns the value 0 to the subscript variable, x. This is done before the while loop is entered because the first item stored in the array is referenced using the subscript value 0. The loop in lines 69 through 73 prints all of the values in the array named score by incrementing the value of the subscript variable, x, each time the loop body executes. When the loop exits, the statement System.exit(0); (line 74) executes and ends the program.

Exercise 8-2: Using a Bubble Sort

In this exercise, you use what you have learned about sorting data using a bubble sort. Study the following code, and then answer Questions 1–4.

```
int numbers[] = {-6, 448, -20, 818, 42, 40, 320, 34};
final int NUM_ITEMS = 8;
int j, k, temp;
int numPasses = 0, numCompares = 0, numSwaps = 0;
for(j = 0; j < NUM_ITEMS - 1; j++)
{
    numPasses++;
    for(k = 0; k < NUM_ITEMS - 1; k++)
    {
        numCompares++;
        if(numbers[k] > numbers[k + 1])
        {
            numSwaps++;
```

```
                    temp = numbers[k + 1];
                    numbers[k + 1] = numbers[k];
                    numbers[k] = temp;
              }
         }
    }
```

1. Does this code perform an ascending sort or a descending sort? How do you know?

   _____

2. How many passes are made over the data in the array?

   _____

3. How many comparisons are made?

   _____

4. Do the variables named `numPasses`, `numCompares`, and `numSwaps` accurately keep track of the number of passes, compares, and swaps made in this bubble sort? Explain your answer.

   _____

LAB 8.2 Using a Bubble Sort

In this lab, you will complete a Java program that uses an array to store data for a computer science teacher. The program is similar to the program described in Chapter 8, Exercise 3 in *Programming Logic and Design, Sixth Edition*. The program should allow the user to enter a student's name and 10 quiz scores. The program should output the student's name and his or her eight highest quiz scores. The file provided for this lab contains the necessary variable declarations and input statements. You need to write the code that sorts the scores in ascending order using a bubble sort, and then prints the student's name and eight highest quiz scores. Comments in the code tell you where to write your statements.

1. Open the source code file named `QuizScores.java` using Notepad or the text editor of your choice.

2. Write the bubble sort.

3. Output the student's name and eight highest quiz scores.

4. Save this source code file in a directory of your choice, and then make that directory your working directory.

5. Compile the source code file, QuizScores.java.

6. Execute the program with the following input, and record the output.

   Student Name: Dan Williams

   Ten Quiz Scores: 75, 32, 78, 92, 80, 77, 92, 92, 86, 99

Using Multidimensional Arrays

As you learned in Chapter 8 of *Programming Logic and Design, Sixth Edition*, an array whose elements are accessed using a single subscript is called a **one-dimensional array** or a **single-dimensional array**. You also learned that a **two-dimensional array** stores elements in two dimensions and requires two subscripts to access elements.

In Chapter 8 of *Programming Logic and Design, Sixth Edition*, you saw how useful two-dimensional arrays can be when you studied the example of owning an apartment building with five floors with each floor having studio, one-bedroom, and two-bedroom apartments. The rent charged for these apartments depends on which floor the apartment is located as well as the number of bedrooms the apartment has. Table 8-1 shows the rental amounts.

Floor	Studio Apartment	1-Bedroom Apartment	2-Bedroom Apartment
0	350	390	435
1	400	440	480
2	475	530	575
3	600	650	700
4	1000	1075	1150

Table 8-1   Rent schedule based on floor and number of bedrooms

In Java, declaring a two-dimensional array to store the rents shown in Table 8-1 requires two sets of square brackets. The first set of square brackets holds the number of rows in the array, and the second set of square brackets holds the number of columns. The declaration is shown below.

```
final int FLOORS = 5;
final int BEDROOMS = 3;
double rent[][] = new double[FLOORS][BEDROOMS];
```

The declaration shows the array's name, `rent`, followed by two sets of empty square brackets. The `new` operator is used to allocate enough memory for the array elements, based on the data type specified and the integer values placed within the two pairs of square brackets that follow the data type. The number of rows is included in the first set of square brackets using the constant value of `FLOORS`(5), and the number of columns is included in the second set of square brackets using the constant value of `BEDROOMS`(3).

As shown below, you can also initialize a two-dimensional array when you declare it by enclosing all of the values within a pair of curly braces and also enclosing the values (separated by commas) for each row within curly braces. Notice that each group of values within curly braces is separated by commas.

```
double rent[][] = {{350, 390, 435},
                   {400, 440, 480},
                   {475, 530, 575},
                   {600, 650, 700},
                   {1000, 1075, 1150}};
```

To access individual elements in the `rent` array, two subscripts are required as shown below.

```
double myRent;
myRent = rent[3][1];
```

Remember that in Java, array subscripts begin with 0.

The first subscript (3) determines the row, and the second subscript (1) determines the column. In the assignment statement, `myRent = rent[3][1]`, the value 650 is assigned to the variable named `myRent`.

Figure 8-3 shows the pseudocode for a program that continuously displays rents for apartments based on renter requests for bedrooms and floor, and Figure 8-4 shows the Java code that implements the program.

```
start
   Declarations
      num RENT_BY_FLOOR_AND_BDRMS[5][3] = {350, 390, 435},
                                          {400, 440, 480},
                                          {475, 530, 575},
                                          {600, 650, 700},
                                          {1000, 1075, 1150}

      num floor
      num bedrooms
      num QUIT = 99
   getReady()
   while floor <> QUIT
```

Figure 8-3   Pseudocode for a program that determines rents *(continues)*

(continued)

```
        determineRent()
    endwhile
    finish()
stop

getReady()
    output "Enter floor "
    input floor
return

determineRent()
    output "Enter number of bedrooms "
    input bedrooms
    output "Rent is $", RENT_BY_FLOOR_AND_BDRMS[floor][bedrooms]
    output "Enter floor "
    input floor
return

finish()
    output "End of program"
return
```

Figure 8-3   Pseudocode for a program that determines rents

```
import javax.swing.*;

public class DetermineRent
{
    public static void main(String args[])
    {
        // Declare variables.
        double rent[][] = {{350, 390, 435},
                           {400, 440, 480},
                           {475, 530, 575},
                           {600, 650, 700},
                           {1000, 1075, 1150}};
        int floor;
        int bedroom;
        String floorString;
        String bedroomString;
        int QUIT = 99;

        // Work done in the getReady() method
        floorString = JOptionPane.showInputDialog(
                    "Enter floor or 99 to quit: ");
        floor = Integer.parseInt(floorString);
```

Figure 8-4   Java code for a program that determines rents *(continues)*

(continued)

```
        while(floor != QUIT)
        {
            // Work done in the determineRent() method
            bedroomString = JOptionPane.showInputDialog(
                        "Enter number of bedrooms: ");
            bedroom = Integer.parseInt(bedroomString);
            System.out.println("Rent is $" +
                            rent[floor][bedroom]);
            floorString = JOptionPane.showInputDialog(
                    "Enter floor or 99 to quit: ");
            floor = Integer.parseInt(floorString);
        }
        // Work done in the finish() method
        System.out.println("End of program");
        System.exit(0);
    } // End of main() method.
} // End of DetermineRent class.
```

Figure 8-4   Java code for a program that determines rents

Exercise 8-3: Using Multidimensional Arrays

In this exercise, you use what you have learned about using multidimensional arrays to answer Questions 1–3.

1. A two-dimensional array declared as
   `int myNums[][] = new int[3][2];` has how many rows?

   _____

2. A two-dimensional array declared as
   `int myNums[][] = new int[3][2];` has how many columns?

   _____

3. Consider the following array declaration,
   `int myNums[][] = new int[3][2];`

   Are the following Java statements legal?

   ```
   number = myNums[3][2];        _____
   number = myNums[0][1];        _____
   number = myNums[1][2];        _____
   ```

LAB 8.3   Using Multidimensional Arrays

In this lab, you will complete a Java program that uses a two-dimensional array to store data for the MidAmerica Bus Company. The program is described in Chapter 8,

Exercise 8 in *Programming Logic and Design, Sixth Edition*. The bus company charges fares to passengers based on the number of travel zones they cross. Additionally, it provides discounts for multiple passengers traveling together. The ticket prices are shown in Table 8-2.

Passengers	Zones Crossed			
	0	**1**	**2**	**3**
1	7.50	10.00	12.00	12.75
2	14.00	18.50	22.00	23.00
3	20.00	21.00	32.00	33.00
4	25.00	27.50	36.00	37.00

Table 8-2 Ticket prices for Lab 8.3

The program should allow users to enter the number of passengers and the number of travel zones they will cross on their bus trip. The program should output the ticket charge. The file provided for this lab contains all of the necessary variable declarations, except the two-dimensional array. You need to write the input statements and the code that initializes the two-dimensional array, determines the ticket charge, and prints the ticket charge. Comments in the code tell you where to write your statements.

1. Open the source code file named Tickets.java using Notepad or the text editor of your choice.

2. Declare and initialize the two-dimensional array.

3. Write the Java statements that retrieve the number of passengers and the number of travel zones crossed.

4. Determine and print the ticket charge.

5. Save this source code file in a directory of your choice, and then make that directory your working directory.

6. Compile the source code file Tickets.java.

7. Execute the program.

CHAPTER 9

Advanced Modularization Techniques

After studying this chapter, you will be able to:

◎ Write methods that require no parameters

◎ Write methods that require a single parameter

◎ Write methods that require multiple parameters

◎ Write methods that return values

◎ Pass entire arrays and single elements of an array to a method

◎ Overload methods

◎ Use Java's built-in methods

In Chapter 2 of *Programming Logic and Design, Sixth Edition*, you learned that local variables are variables that are declared within the method that uses them. You also learned that most programs consist of a main method, which contains the mainline logic and calls other methods to get specific work done in the program.

In this chapter, you learn more about methods in Java. You learn how to write methods that require no parameters, how to write methods that require a single parameter, how to write methods that require multiple parameters, and how to write methods that return a value. You also learn how to pass an array to a method, how to overload a method, and how to use some of Java's built-in methods. To help you learn about methods, you will study some Java programs that implement the logic and design presented in *Programming Logic and Design, Sixth Edition*.

You should do the exercises and labs in this chapter after you have finished Chapter 9 of *Programming Logic and Design, Sixth Edition*.

Writing Methods with No Parameters

To begin learning about methods, we review the Java code for a Customer Bill program, shown in Figure 9-1. Notice the line numbers in front of each line of code in this program. These line numbers are not actually part of the program but are included for reference only.

```
1 import javax.swing.JOptionPane;
2 public class CustomerBill
3 {
4     public static void main(String args[])
5     {
6        // Declare variables local to main()
7        String name;
8        String balanceString;
9        double balance;
10
11       // Get interactive input
12       name = JOptionPane.showInputDialog(
13                   "Enter customer's name: ");
14       balanceString = JOptionPane.showInputDialog(
15                   "Enter customer's balance: ");
16
17       // Convert String to double
18       balance = Double.parseDouble(balanceString);
19
20       // Call nameAndAddress() method
```

Figure 9-1   Java code for the Customer Bill program *(continues)*

(continued)

```
21        nameAndAddress();
22
23        // Output customer name and address
24        System.out.println("Customer Name: " + name);
25        System.out.println("Customer Balance: " + balance);
26
27    }
28    public static void nameAndAddress()
29    {
30        // Declare and initialize local, constant Strings
31        final String ADDRESS_LINE1 = "ABC Manufacturing";
32        final String ADDRESS_LINE2 = "47 Industrial Lane";
33        final String ADDRESS_LINE3 = "Wild Rose, WI 54984";
34
35        // Output
36        System.out.println(ADDRESS_LINE1);
37        System.out.println(ADDRESS_LINE2);
38        System.out.println(ADDRESS_LINE3);
39    } // End of nameAndAddress() method
40 }
```

Figure 9-1   Java code for the Customer Bill program

The program begins execution with the main() method, which is shown on line 4. This method contains the declaration of three variables (lines 7, 8, and 9), name, balanceString, and balance, which are local to the main() method. Next, on lines 12, 13, 14, and 15, interactive input statements retrieve values for name and balanceString, and on line 18 balanceString is converted to the double data type. The method nameAndAddress() is then called on line 21, with no arguments listed within its parentheses. **Arguments**, which are sometimes called **actual parameters**, are data items sent to methods. There are no arguments for the nameAndAddress() method because this method requires no data. You will learn about passing arguments to methods later in this chapter. The last two statements (lines 24 and 25) in the main() method are print statements that output the customer's name and balance.

Next, on line 28, you see the header for the nameAndAddress() method. The **header** begins with the public keyword, followed by the static keyword, followed by the void keyword, followed by the method name, which is nameAndAddress(). The public keyword makes this method available for execution. The keyword static means you do not have to create a CustomerBill object to call the method, and the void keyword indicates that the nameAndAddress() method does not return a value. You learn more about methods that return values later in this chapter. When the input to this program is Ed Gonzales (name) and 352.39 (balance), the output is shown in Figure 9-2.

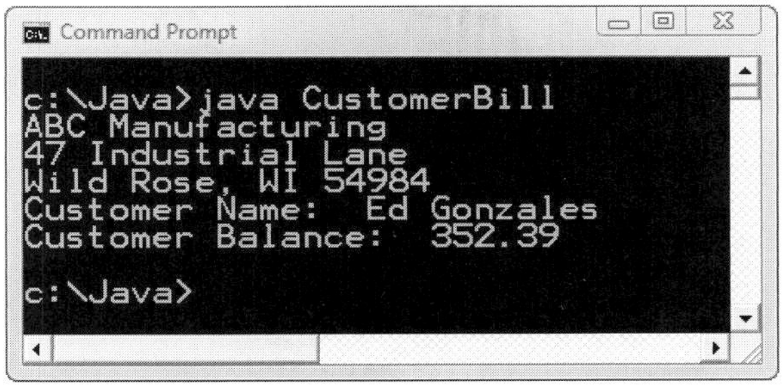

Figure 9-2 Output from the Customer Bill program

Exercise 9-1: Writing Methods with No Parameters

In this exercise, you use what you have learned about writing methods with no parameters to answer Questions 1–2.

1. Given the following method calls, write the method's header:

   a. `printBusinessCard();`

      _____

   b. `displayCustomerInfo();`

      _____

   c. `displayRecipe();`

      _____

2. Given the following method headers, write a method call:

   a. `public static void displayStudentAddress()`

      _____

   b. `public static void printRoster()`

      _____

   c. `public static void displayEmployeeNames()`

      _____

155

LAB 9.1   Writing Methods with No Parameters

In this lab, you complete a partially prewritten Java program that includes a method with no parameters. The program prompts the user for his or her age. If the user is 18 or older, the program should call a method named `canVote()` that displays the message "You are old enough to vote in this election." If the user is younger than 18, the program should call a method named `cannotVote()` that displays the message "Sorry, you'll have to wait to vote until you are 18." The source code file provided for this lab includes the necessary variable declarations and the input statement. Comments are included in the file to help you write the remainder of the program.

1. Open the source code file named `AllowVote.java` using Notepad or the text editor of your choice.

2. Write the Java statements as indicated by the comments.

3. Save this source code file in a directory of your choice, and then make that directory your working directory.

4. Compile the source code file, `AllowVote.java`.

5. Execute the program.

Writing Methods that Require a Single Parameter

As you learned in *Programming Logic and Design, Sixth Edition*, some methods require data to accomplish their task. You also learned that designing a program so that it sends data (which can be different each time the program runs) to a method (which doesn't change) keeps you from having to write multiple methods to handle similar situations. For example, suppose you are writing a program that has to determine if a number is even or odd. It is certainly better to write a single method, to which the program can pass a number entered by the user, than to write individual methods for every number.

In Figure 9-3, you see the Java code for a program that includes a method that can determine if a number is odd or even. The line numbers are not actually part of the program but are included for reference only. The program allows the user to enter a number, and then passes that number to a method as an argument. After it receives the argument, the method can determine if the number is an even number or an odd number.

```
1 // EvenOrOdd.java - This program determines if a number
2 // input by the user is an even number or an odd number.
3 // Input:  Interactive.
4 // Output: The number entered and whether it is even or odd.
5
6 import javax.swing.*;
7
8 public class EvenOrOdd
9 {
10    public static void main(String args[])
11    {
12       int number;
13       String numberString;
14
15       numberString = JOptionPane.showInputDialog(
16             "Enter a number or -999 to quit: ");
17       number= Integer.parseInt(numberString);
18
19       while(number != -999)
20       {
21          even_or_odd(number);
22          numberString = JOptionPane.showInputDialog(
23                "Enter a number or -999 to quit: ");
24          number= Integer.parseInt(numberString);
25       }
26
27       System.exit(0);
28
29    } // End of main() method.
30
31    public static void even_or_odd(int number)
32    {
33       if((number % 2) == 0)
34          System.out.println("Number: " + number +
35                         " is even.");
36       else
37          System.out.println("Number: " + number +
38                         " is odd.");
39    } // End of even_or_odd method
40 } // End of EvenOrOdd class.
```

The variable named **number** is local to the **main()** method. Its value is stored at one memory location. For example, it may be stored at memory location 2000.

The value of the formal parameter, **number**, is stored at a different memory location and is local to the **even_or_odd()** method. For example, it may be stored at memory location 7800.

Figure 9-3   Java code for the Even Or Odd program

On lines 15 and 16 in this program, the user is asked to enter a number or the sentinel value, -999, when she is finished entering numbers and wants to quit the program. (You learned about sentinel values in Chapter 5 of this book.) On lines 15, 16, and 17, the input value is retrieved, stored in the variable named numberString, converted to an int, and then stored in the variable named number. Next, if the user did not enter the sentinel value -999, the while loop is entered, and the method named even_or_odd() is called (line 21) using the following syntax, even_or_odd(number);.

Notice that the variable, number, is placed within the parentheses on line 21, which means that the value of number is passed to the even_or_odd() method. This is referred to as passing an argument by value. **Passing an argument by value** means that a copy of the value of the argument is passed to the method. Within the method, the value is stored in the formal parameter at a different memory location, and is considered local to that method. In this example, as shown on line 31, the value is stored in the formal parameter named number.

The data type of the formal parameter and the actual parameter must be the same.

Program control is now transferred to the even_or_odd() method. The header for the even_or_odd() method on line 31 includes the public, static, and void keywords, as discussed earlier in this chapter. The name of the method follows, and within the parentheses that follow the method name, the parameter, number, is given a local name and declared as the int data type.

Remember that even though the name of the parameter, number, has the same name as the local variable number in the main() method, they are stored at different memory locations. Figure 9-3 shows that the variable number that is local to main() is stored at one memory location, and the parameter, number, in the even_or_odd() method is stored at a different memory location.

Within the method on line 33, the modulus operator, %, is used in the test portion of the if statement to determine if the value of the local number is even or odd. The user is then informed if number is even (lines 34 and 35) or odd (lines 37 and 38), and program control is transferred back to the statement that follows the call to even_or_odd() in the main() method (line 22).

Back in the main() method, the user is asked to enter another number on lines 22 and 23, and the while loop continues to execute, calling the even_or_odd() method with a new input value. The loop is exited when the user enters the sentinel value −999, and the program ends. When the input to this program is 45, 98, 1, −32, 643, and −999, the output is shown in Figure 9-4.

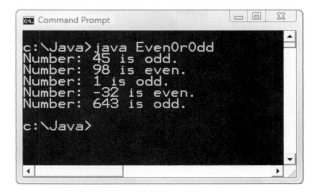

Figure 9-4 Output from the Even Or Odd program

Exercise 9-2: Writing Methods that Require a Single Parameter

In this exercise, you use what you have learned about writing methods that require a single parameter to answer Questions 1–2.

1. Given the following variable declarations and method calls, write the method's header:

    a. `String name;`

    `printNameBadge(name);`

    _____

    b. `double side_length;`

    `calculateRectangleArea(side_length);`

    _____

    c. `int hours;`

    `displaySecondsInHours(hours);`

    _____

2. Given the following method headers, write a method call:

    a. `public static void displayPetName(String petName)`

    _____

    b. `public static void printHolidays(int year)`

    _____

    c. `public static void checkValidPassword(String password)`

    _____

LAB 9.2 Writing Methods that Require a Single Parameter

In this lab, you complete a partially written Java program that includes a method requiring a single parameter. The program prompts the user for an integer. If the integer is divisible by 9, the program calls a method named divideByNine(). This method displays the message "number divided by 9 is result", where number is the value of number and result is the value of result. If the number is not divisible by 9, the message "Sorry, number is not divisible by 9" is displayed, where number is the value of number. The source code file provided for this lab includes the necessary variable declarations and the input statement. Comments are included in the file to help you write the remainder of the program.

1. Open the source code file named DivideByNine.java using Notepad or the text editor of your choice.

2. Write the Java statements as indicated by the comments.

3. Save this source code file in a directory of your choice, and then make that directory your working directory.

4. Compile the source code file, DivideByNine.java.

5. Execute the program.

Writing Methods that Require Multiple Parameters

In Chapter 9 of *Programming Logic and Design, Sixth Edition*, you learned that a method often requires more than one parameter in order to accomplish its task. To specify that a method requires multiple parameters, you include a list of data types and local identifiers separated by commas as part of the method's header. To call a method that expects multiple parameters, you list the actual parameters (separated by commas) in the call to the method.

In Figure 9-5, you see the Java code for a program that includes a method named computeTax() that you designed in *Programming Logic and Design, Sixth Edition*. The line numbers are not actually part of the program but are included for reference only.

```
 1 // ComputeTax.java - This program computes tax given a
 2 // balance and a rate
 3 // Input:  Interactive.
 4 // Output:  The balance, tax rate, and computed tax.
 5
 6 import javax.swing.*;
 7
 8 public class ComputeTax
 9 {
10    public static void main(String args[])
11    {
12       double balance;                                    Memory address 1000
13       String balanceString;
14       double rate;                                       Memory address 1008
15       String rateString;
16
17       balanceString = JOptionPane.showInputDialog(
18                       "Enter balance: ");
19       balance = Double.parseDouble(balanceString);
20       rateString = JOptionPane.showInputDialog(
21                    "Enter rate: ");
22       rate = Double.parseDouble(rateString);
23
24       computeTax(balance, rate);
25
26       System.exit(0);
27                                                          Memory address 9000
28    } // End of main() method.
29
30    public static void computeTax(double amount, double rate)
31    {                                                     Memory address 9008
32       double tax;
33
34       tax = amount * rate;
35       System.out.println("Amount: " + amount + " Rate: " +
36                          rate + " Tax: " + tax);
37
38    } // End of computeTax method
39 } // End of ComputeTax class.
```

Figure 9-5 Java code for the Compute Tax program

In the Java code shown in Figure 9-5, you see that the highlighted call
to computeTax() on line 24 includes the names of the local variables
balance and rate within the parentheses and that they are separated
by a comma. These are the arguments (actual parameters) that are
passed to the computeTax() method. You can also see that the
computeTax() method header on line 30 is highlighted and includes
two formal parameters, double amount and double rate, listed within
parentheses and separated by a comma. The value of the variable
named balance is passed by value to the computeTax() method as

an actual parameter and is stored in the formal parameter named `amount`. The value of the variable named `rate` is passed by value to the `computeTax()` method as an actual parameter and is stored in the formal parameter named `rate`. As illustrated in Figure 9-5, it does not matter that one of the parameters being passed, `rate`, has the same name as the parameter received, `rate`, because they occupy different memory locations. When the input to this program is 300.00 (balance) and .12 (rate), the output is shown in Figure 9-6.

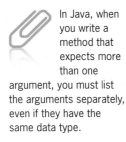
In Java, when you write a method that expects more than one argument, you must list the arguments separately, even if they have the same data type.

Figure 9-6   Output from the Compute Tax program

Exercise 9-3: Writing Methods that Require Multiple Parameters

In this exercise, you use what you have learned about writing methods that require multiple parameters to answer Questions 1–2.

There is no limit to the number of arguments you can pass to a method, but when multiple arguments are passed to a method, the call to the method and the method's header must match. This means that the number of arguments, their data types, and the order in which they are listed must be the same.

1.   Given the following method calls, write the method's header:

a.   `String name, title;`

   `printNameBadge(name, title);`

   _____

b.   `double one_length, two_length;`

   `calculateSquareArea(one_length, two_length);`

   _____

c.   `int day, month, year;`

   `double amount;`

   `printBill(day, month, year, amount);`

   _____

2. Given the following method headers, write a method call:

    a. `public static void studentInfo(String name, double tuition)`

    _____

    b. `public static void printProduct(int num1, int num2)`

    _____

    c. `public static void decrease(double bal, double payment)`

    _____

LAB 9.3 Writing Methods that Require Multiple Parameters

In this lab, you complete a partially written Java program that includes a method requiring multiple parameters (arguments). The program prompts the user for an item price and the number of items ordered. If the item's price is less than $5.00, the program should apply a 4% discount; if the item's price is between $5.00 and $9.99, the program should apply a 7% discount; if the item is $10.00 or more, the program should apply a 10% discount. Once the discount is applied, the program should calculate the total price for the number of items purchased and then display the original price, the discount percent, the discounted price, the quantity ordered, and the total price for the items ordered. The source code file provided for this lab includes the variable declarations and the input statements. Comments are included in the file to help you write the remainder of the program.

1. Open the source code file named `DiscountPrices.java` using Notepad or the text editor of your choice.

2. Write the Java statements as indicated by the comments.

3. Save this source code file in a directory of your choice, and then make that directory your working directory.

4. Compile the source code file, `DiscountPrices.java`.

5. Execute the program.

Writing Methods that Return a Value

Thus far in this book, none of the methods you have written return a value. The header for each of these methods includes the keyword void, as in, public static void main(), indicating that the method does not return a value. However, as a programmer, you will often find that you need to write methods that do return a value. In Java, a method can only return a single value; when you write the code for the method, you must indicate the data type of the value you want to return. This is often referred to as the method's return type. The return type can be any of Java's built-in data types, as well as a class type, such as String. You will learn more about classes in Chapter 10 of this book. For now, we will focus on returning values of the built-in types and String objects.

In Chapter 9 of *Programming Logic and Design, Sixth Edition*, you studied the design for a program that includes a method named getHoursWorked(). This method is designed to prompt a user for the number of hours an employee has worked, retrieve the value, and then return that value to the location in the program where the method was called. The Java code that implements this design in shown in Figure 9-7.

```
1 // GrossPay.java - This program computes an employee's
2 // gross pay.
3 // Input:  Interactive.
4 // Output:  The employee's hours worked and their gross pay.
5
6 import javax.swing.*;
7
8 public class GrossPay
9 {
10     public static void main(String args[])
11     {
12         double hours;
13         final double PAY_RATE = 12.00;
14         double gross;
15
16         hours = getHoursWorked();
17         gross = hours * PAY_RATE;
18
19         System.out.println("Hours worked: " + hours);
20         System.out.println("Gross pay is: " + gross);
21
22         System.exit(0);
23
24     } // End of main() method.
```

Figure 9-7 Java code for a program that includes the getHoursWorked() method *(continues)*

(continued)

```
25
26     public static double getHoursWorked()
27     {
28        double workHours;
29        String workHoursString;
30
31        workHoursString = JOptionPane.showInputDialog(
32                "Please enter hours worked: ");
33        workHours = Double.parseDouble(workHoursString);
34
35        return workHours;
36
37     } // End of getHoursWorked method
38 } // End of GrossPay class.
```

Figure 9-7   Java code for a program that includes the `getHoursWorked()` method

The Java program shown in Figure 9-7 declares local constants and variables hours, PAY_RATE, and gross on lines 12, 13, and 14 in the main() method. The next statement (line 16), shown below, is an assignment statement.

```
hours = getHoursWorked();
```

This assignment statement includes a call to the method named getHoursWorked(). As with all assignment statements, the expression on the right side of the assignment operator (=) is evaluated, and then the result is assigned to the variable named on the left side of the assignment operator (=). In this example, the expression on the right is a call to the getHoursWorked() method.

When the getHoursWorked() method is called, program control is transferred to the method. Notice that the header (line 26) for this method is written as follows:

```
public static double getHoursWorked()
```

The keyword double is used in the header to specify that a value of data type double is returned by this method.

Two local variables, workHours (data type double) and workHoursString (a String object), are then declared on lines 28 and 29. On lines 31 and 32, the user is then asked to enter the number of hours worked, at which point the value is retrieved and stored in workHoursString. Next, on line 33, workHoursString is converted to a double, and assigned to the local variable named workHours. The return statement that follows on line 35 returns a copy of the value stored in workHours (data type double) to the location in the calling method where getHoursWorked() is called, which is the right side of the assignment statement on line 16.

The value returned to the right side of the assignment statement is then assigned to the variable named hours (data type double) in the main() method. Next, the gross pay is calculated on line 17, followed by the System.out.println() statements on lines 19 and 20 that display the value of the local variables, hours and gross, which contain the number of hours worked and the calculated gross pay.

You can also use a method's return value directly rather than store it in a variable. The two Java statements that follow make calls to the same getHoursWorked() method shown in Figure 9-7, but in these statements the returned value is used directly in the statement that calculates gross pay and in the statement that prints the returned value.

```
gross = getHoursWorked() * PAY_RATE;
System.out.println("Hours worked is " + getHoursWorked());
```

When the input to this program is 45, the output is shown in Figure 9-8.

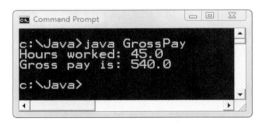

Figure 9-8   Output from program that includes the getHoursWorked() method

Exercise 9-4: Writing Methods that Return a Value

In this exercise, you use what you have learned about writing methods that return a value to answer Questions 1–2.

1. Given the following variable declarations and method calls, write the method's header:

    a. `double price, percent, newPrice;`

    `newPrice = calculatePriceIncrease(price, percent);`

    _____

    b. `double area, one_length, two_length;`

    `area = figureArea(one_length, two_length);`

    _____

c. String lower_case, upper_case;

upper_case = changeCase(lower_case);

_____

2. Given the following method headers, write a method call:

a. public static String findCustomerType(int custNumber)

_____

b. public static int product(int num1, int num2)

_____

c. public static int power(int num, int exp)

_____

LAB 9.4 Writing Methods that Return a Value

In this lab, you complete a partially written Java program that includes a method that returns a value. The program is a simple calculator that prompts the user for two numbers and an operator (+, -, *, /, or %). The two numbers and the operator are passed to the method where the appropriate arithmetic operation is performed. The result is then returned to the main() method where the arithmetic operation and result are displayed. For example, if the user enters 3, 4, and *, the following is displayed:

3.00 * 4.00 = 12.00

The source code file provided for this lab includes the necessary variable declarations, and input and output statements. Comments are included in the file to help you write the remainder of the program.

1. Open the source code file named Arithmetic.java using Notepad or the text editor of your choice.

2. Write the Java statements as indicated by the comments.

3. Save this source code file in a directory of your choice, and then make that directory your working directory.

4. Compile the source code file, Arithmetic.java.

5. Execute the program.

Passing an Array and an Array Element to a Method

As a Java programmer, there are times when you will want to write a method that will perform a task on all of the elements you have stored in an array. For example, in Chapter 9 of *Programming Logic and Design, Sixth Edition*, you saw a design for a program that used a method to quadruple all of the values stored in an array. This design is translated into Java code in Figure 9-9.

The `main()` method begins on line 4 and proceeds with the declaration and initialization of the constant named LENGTH (line 7) and the array of integers named someNums (line 8), followed by the declaration of the variable named x (line 9), which is used as a loop control variable. The first `while` loop in the program on lines 12 through 16 prints the values stored in the array at the beginning of the program. On line 18, the method named `quadrupleTheValues()` is called. The array named someNums is passed as an argument.

```
 1 import javax.swing.*;
 2 public class PassEntireArray
 3 {
 4    public static void main(String args[])
 5    {
 6       // Declare variables
 7       final int LENGTH = 4;
 8       int someNums[]= {10, 12, 22, 35};
 9       int x;
10       System.out.println("At beginning of main method...");
11       x = 0;
12       while (x < LENGTH) // Print initial array values
13       {
14          System.out.println(someNums[x]);
15          x++;
16       }
17       // Call method, pass array
18       quadrupleTheValues(someNums);
19       System.out.println("At the end of main method...");
20       x = 0;
21       // Print changed array values
22       while (x < someNums.length)
23       {
24          System.out.println(someNums[x]);
25          x ++;
26       }
27       System.exit(0);
28    } // End of main() method.
```

Figure 9-9   Java code for the Pass Entire Array program *(continues)*

(continued)

```
29     public static void quadrupleTheValues(int [] vals)
30     {
31        final int LENGTH = 4;
32        int x;
33        x = 0;
34        // Print array values before they are changed
35        while(x < LENGTH)
36        {
37           System.out.println(
38              " In quadrupleTheValues() method, value is " +
39              vals[x]);
40           x++;
41        }
42        x = 0;
43        while(x < LENGTH) // This loop changes array values
44        {
45           vals[x] = vals[x] * 4;
46           x++;
47        }
48        x = 0;
49        // Print array values after they are changed
50        while(x < LENGTH)
51        {
52           System.out.println(" After change, value is " +
53              vals[x]);
54           x++;
55        }
56     } // End of quadrupleTheValues method
57 } // End of PassEntireArray class.
```

Figure 9-9 Java code for the Pass Entire Array program

When an entire array is passed to a method, the square brackets and the size are not included. Note that when you pass an entire array to a method, the array is **passed by reference**. So, instead of a copy of the array being passed, the memory address of the array is passed. This gives the method access to that memory location; the method can then change the values stored in the array if necessary.

Program control is then transferred to the quadrupleTheValues() method. The header for the method on line 29 includes one parameter, int [] vals. The syntax for declaring an array as a formal parameter includes the parameter's data type, followed by empty square brackets, followed by a local name for the array. Note that a size is not included within the square brackets. In the quadrupleTheValues() method, the first while loop on lines 35 through 41 prints the values stored in the array, and the second while loop on lines 43 through 47 accesses each element in the array, quadruples the value, and then stores the quadrupled values in the array at their same location. The third `while` loop on lines 50 through 55 prints the changed values now stored in the array. Program control is then returned to the location in the `main()` method where the method was called.

When program control returns to the `main()` method, the next statements to execute (lines 19 through 26) are responsible for printing out the values stored in the array once more. The output from this program is displayed in Figure 9-10.

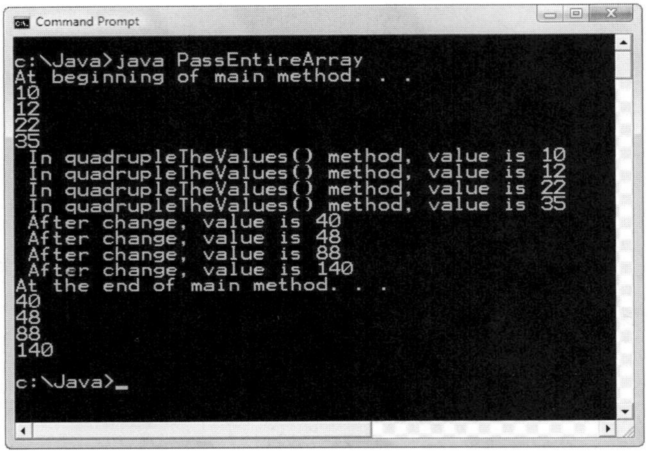

Figure 9-10   Output from the Pass Entire Array program

As shown in Figure 9-10, the array values printed at the beginning of the `main()` method (lines 12 through 16) are the values with which the array was initialized. Next, the `quadrupleTheValues()` method prints the array values (lines 35 through 41) again before they are changed. The values remain the same as the initialized values. The `quadrupleTheValues()` method then prints the array values again after the values are quadrupled (lines 50 through 55). After the call to `quadrupleTheValues()`, the `main()` method prints the array values one last time (lines 22 through 26). These are the quadrupled values, indicating that the `quadrupleTheValues()` method has access to the memory location where the array is stored and can permanently change the values stored there.

You can also pass a single array element to a method, just as you pass a variable or constant. The following Java code initializes an array named `someNums`, declares a variable named `newNum`, and passes one element of the array to a method named `tripleTheNumber()`.

```
int someNums[]= {10, 12, 22, 35};
int newNum;
newNum = tripleTheNumber(someNums[1]);
```

The following Java code includes the header for the method named
tripleTheNumber() along with the code that triples the value passed to it.

```
public static int tripleTheNumber(int num)
{
    int result;
    result = num * 3;
    return result;
}
```

Exercise 9-5: Passing Arrays to Methods

In this exercise, you use what you have learned about passing arrays
and array elements to methods to answer Questions 1–3.

1. Given the following method calls, write the method's header:

   a. `int septemberDueDates [] = {3, 12, 13, 22, 27, 30};`

       `printDueDates(septemberDueDates);`

       _____

   b. `double febInvoices [] = {100.00, 200.00, 55.00, 230.00};`

       `total = monthlyIncome(febInvoices);`

       _____

   c. `double overdue[] = {34.56, 33.22, 65.77, 89.99};`

       `printNotice(overdue[1]);`

       _____

2. Given the following method headers, write a method call:

   a. `public static void Student(String [] name,`
       `double [] grades)`

       _____

   b. `public static int printAverage(int [] nums )`

       _____

3. Given the following method header (in which sal is one
   element of an array of doubles), write a method call:

   a. `public static void increase(double sal)`

       _____

LAB 9.5 Passing Arrays to Methods

In this lab, you complete a partially written Java program that prints student grade reports. The program passes two parallel arrays to a method where grade reports are printed. One array contains doubles that represent a student's numeric grade average; the second array contains the names of students, stored as Strings. The method prints the student's name followed by his or her letter grade, as shown below.

Name: Maria Frederick – Grade: A

In this program, a student earns letter grades as shown in Table 9-1:

Numeric Grade	Letter Grade
90–100	A
80–89	B
70–79	C
60–69	D
Less than 60	F

Table 9-1 Numeric and letter grades

The source code file provided for this lab includes the necessary variable declarations. Comments are included in the file to help you write the remainder of the program.

1. Open the source code file named StudentGrades.java using Notepad or the text editor of your choice.

2. Write the Java statements as indicated by the comments.

3. Save this source code file in a directory of your choice, and then make that directory your working directory.

4. Compile the source code file, StudentGrades.java.

5. Execute the program.

Overloading Methods

You can **overload** methods by giving the same name to more than one method. Overloading methods is useful when you need to perform the same action on different types of inputs. For example, you may want to write multiple versions of an add() method—one that can add two integers, another that can add two doubles, another that can add three integers, and another that can add two integers and a double. Overloaded methods have the same name, but they must either have a different number of arguments or the arguments must be of a different data type. Java figures out which method to call based on the method's name and its arguments, the combination of which is known as the method's **signature**. The signature of an overloaded method consists of the method's name and its argument list; it does not include the method's return type.

Overloading methods allows a Java programmer to choose a meaningful name for a method and also permits the use of polymorphic code. **Polymorphic** code is code that acts appropriately depending on the context. (The word polymorphic is derived from the Greek words *poly*, meaning "many," and *morph*, meaning "form.") Polymorphic methods in Java can take many forms. You will learn more about polymorphism in other Java courses, when you learn more about object-oriented programming. For now, you can use overloading to write methods that perform the same task but with different data types.

In Chapter 9 of *Programming Logic and Design, Sixth Edition*, you studied the design for an overloaded method named printBill(). One version of the method includes a numeric parameter, a second version includes two numeric parameters, a third version includes a numeric parameter and a String parameter, and a fourth version includes two numeric parameters and a String parameter. All versions of the printBill() method have the same name with a different signature; therefore, it is an overloaded method. In Figure 9-11 you see a Java program that includes the four versions of the printBill() method.

```
1 // Overloaded.java - This program illustrates overloaded
2 // methods.
3 // Input:   None.
4 // Output:  Bill printed in various ways.
5 import javax.swing.*;
6 public class Overloaded
7 {
8    public static void main(String args[])
9    {
10       double bal = 250.00, discountRate = .05;
11       String msg = "Due in 10 days.";
12       printBill(bal);                          // Call version #1
13       printBill(bal, discountRate);            // Call version #2
14       printBill(bal, msg);                     // Call version #3
15       printBill(bal, discountRate, msg);       // Call version #4
16       System.exit(0);
17    } // End of main() method.
18
```

Figure 9-11   Program that uses overloaded printBill() methods *(continues)*

(continued)

```
19    // printBill() method version #1
20    public static void printBill(double balance)
21    {
22       System.out.println("Thank you for your order.");
23       System.out.println("Please remit " + balance);
24    } // End of printBill version #1 method
25
26    // printBill() method version #2
27    public static void printBill(double balance,
28                                       double discount)
29    {
30       double newBal;
31       newBal = balance - (balance * discount);
32       System.out.println("Thank you for your order.");
33       System.out.println("Please remit " + newBal);
34    } // End of printBill version #2 method
35
36    // printBill() method version #3
37    public static void printBill(double balance,
38                                       String message)
39    {
40       System.out.println("Thank you for your order.");
41       System.out.println(message);
42       System.out.println("Please remit " + balance);
43    } // End of printBill version #3 method
44
45    // printBill() method version #4
46    public static void printBill(double balance,
47                                       double discount,
48                                       String message)
49    {
50       double  newBal;
51       newBal = balance - (balance * discount);
52       System.out.println("Thank you for your order.");
53       System.out.println(message);
54       System.out.println("Please remit " + newBal);
55    } // End of printBill version #4 method
56 } // End of Overloaded class.
```

Figure 9-11   Program that uses overloaded `printBill()` methods

On line 12, the first call to the `printBill()` method passes one argument, the variable named `bal`, which is declared as a `double`. This causes the run-time system to find and execute the `printBill()` method that is written to accept one `double` as an argument (line 20). The third call to the `printBill()` method (line 14) passes two arguments, a `double` and a `String`. This causes the run-time system to find and execute the `printBill()` method that is written to accept a `double` and a `String` as arguments (line 37). You can compile and execute this program if you would like to verify that a different version of the printBill() method is called when a different number of arguments are passed or arguments of different data types are passed. The program, named Overloaded.java, is included with the data files provided with this book. The output generated by this program is shown in Figure 9-12.

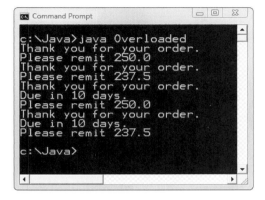

Figure 9-12 Output from the Overloaded program

Exercise 9-6: Overloading Methods

In this exercise, you use what you have learned about overloading methods to answer Question 1.

1. In Figure 9-13, which method header would the following method calls match? Use a line number as your answer.

a. ans2 = sum(2.0,5.0);

_____

b. ans1 = sum(2, 5);

_____

c. ans1 = sum(number1, number1);

_____

d. ans2 = sum(3, 5, 7);

_____

e. ans2 = sum(2, 4, number2);

_____

```
1 // Method headers
2 public static int sum(int num1, int num2)
3 public static int sum(int num2, int num2, int num3)
4 public static double sum(double num1, double num2)
5 double number1 = 1.0, ans1;
6 int number2 = 5, ans2;
```

Figure 9-13   Method headers for Exercise 9-6

LAB 9.6   Overloading Methods

In this lab, you complete a partially written Java program that includes overloaded methods. The program is written to check if a student provided correct answers on a test. The test included three questions. One question requires an `int` for the answer, one question requires a `String` for the answer, and another question requires a `boolean` for the answer. The source code file provided for this lab includes variable declarations that are initialized with a student's answers. It also includes the necessary output statements. You must write three overloaded methods named `checkQuestion()`. One of the methods should accept an `int` argument that represents the student's `int` answer, one should accept a `String` argument that represents the student's `String` answer, and one should accept a `boolean` argument that represents the student's `boolean` answer. In the methods, you should test for correct answers and return the value "Correct" or "Incorrect". The correct `int` answer is 2, the correct `String` answer is "Abraham Lincoln", and the correct `boolean` answer is `false`. Comments are included in the file to help you write the remainder of the program.

1. Open the source code file named `CheckAnswer.java` using Notepad or the text editor of your choice.

2. Write the Java statements as indicated by the comments.

3. Save this source code file in a directory of your choice, and then make that directory your working directory.

4. Compile the source code file, `CheckAnswer.java`.

5. Execute the program.

Using Java's Built-In Methods

Throughout this book, you have used some of Java's built-in methods, such as the `println()` method, the `showInputDialog()` method, and the `parseInt()` and `parseDouble()` methods. In this section, we will look at another built-in method named `format()`, which allows you to control the number of places displayed after the decimal point when you print a value of data type `double`. Using the `format()` method is one of several ways to control the number of places displayed after a decimal point.

In the code sample that follows, you see that the `format()` method expects two arguments, a string constant and a value to format. Notice the value to format is a variable named `valToFormat` that is declared as data type `double`.

```
double valToFormat = 1234.12;
System.out.format("%.3f%n", valToFormat);
```

In the preceding code sample, the `String` constant, "%.3f%n", is a format **specifier** that describes how the value should be formatted. Format specifiers begin with a percent sign (%) and end with a converter. The **converter** is a character indicating the type of argument to be formatted. In this example, the `f` in `%.3f` specifies that the value to be formatted is a floating-point value. In between the percent sign (%) and the converter, you can include optional flags and specifiers. In this example, `.3` is an optional flag that specifies that you want to display three places after the decimal point. The format specifier, `%n`, indicates that a newline character should be displayed. The output from this code sample is 1234.120.

As you continue to learn more about Java, you will be introduced to many more built-in methods that you can use in your programs.

Exercise 9-7: Using Java's Built-In Methods

In this exercise, you use the online documentation supplied by Sun to answer Questions 1–8. Go to *http://java.sun.com/javase/6/docs/api* to access Java's online documentation. Scroll down until you see the word String in the left pane, under "All Classes." Click String to access the documentation regarding Java's `String` class. Read the information about the built-in methods that belong to the `String` class, and then answer the following questions:

1. What does the `endsWith()` method do?

2. What data type does the endsWith() method return?

_____

3. What does the charAt() method do?

_____

4. What data type does the charAt() method return?

_____

5. How many arguments does the charAt() method require?

_____

6. What is the data type of the argument(s)?

_____

7. Is the valueOf() method overloaded?

_____

8. How many versions of the valueOf() method are listed?

_____

LAB 9.7   Using Java's Built-In Methods

In this lab, you complete a partially written Java program that includes built-in methods that convert Strings to all uppercase or all lowercase. The program prompts the user to enter any String. To end the program, the user can enter "done". For each String entered, call the built-in methods toLowerCase() and toUpperCase(). The program should call these methods using a String object, followed by a dot (.), followed by the name of the method. Both of these methods return a String with the String changed to uppercase or lowercase. Here is an example:

```
String sample = "This is a String.";
String result;
result = sample.toLowerCase();
result = sample.toUpperCase();
```

The source code file provided for this lab includes the necessary variable declarations and the necessary input and output statements. Comments are included in the file to help you write the remainder of the program.

1. Open the source code file named `ChangeCase.java` using Notepad or the text editor of your choice.

2. Write the Java statements as indicated by the comments.

3. Save this source code file in a directory of your choice, and then make that directory your working directory.

4. Compile the source code file, `ChangeCase.java`.

5. Execute the program.

Additional Topics

After studying this chapter, you will be able to:

- ◎ Create a simple programmer-defined class
- ◎ Create a simple Graphical User Interface (GUI)

This chapter covers topics included in Chapters 10, 11, and 12 in *Programming Logic and Design, Sixth Edition*, by Joyce Farrell.

A Programmer-Defined Class

You should do the exercises and labs in this section after you have finished Chapters 10 and 11 in *Programming Logic and Design, Sixth Edition.* You should also take a moment to review the object-oriented terminology (class, attribute, and method) presented in Chapter 1 of this book and in Chapter 10 of *Programming Logic and Design, Sixth Edition.*

You have been using prewritten classes, objects, and methods throughout this book. For example, you have used the `showInputDialog()` method that belongs to the `JOptionPane` class to display an input dialog box, and you have used the `parseInt()` method that belongs to the `Integer` class. In this section, you learn how to create your own class that includes attributes and methods of your choice. In programming terminology, a class created by the programmer is referred to as a **programmer-defined class**.

To review, procedural programming focuses on declaring data and defining methods separate from the data and then calling those methods to operate on the data. This is the style of programming you have been using in Chapters 1 through 9 of this book. Object-oriented programming is different from procedural programming. Object-oriented programming focuses on an application's data and the methods you need to manipulate that data. The data and methods are **encapsulated**, or contained within, a class. Objects are created as an instance of a class. The program tells an object to perform tasks by passing messages to it. Such a message consists of an instruction to execute one of the class's methods. The class method then manipulates the data (which is part of the object itself).

Creating a Programmer-Defined Class

In Chapter 10 of *Programming Logic and Design, Sixth Edition,* you studied pseudocode for the Employee class. This pseudocode is shown in Figure 10-1. The Java code that implements the Employee class is shown in Figure 10-2.

```
1 class Employee
2     string lastName
3     num hourlyWage
4     num weeklyPay
5
6     void setLastName(string name)
7         lastName = name
8     return
9
10    void setHourlyWage(num wage)
11        hourlyWage = wage
12        calculateWeeklyPay()
13    return
14
15    string getLastName()
16    return lastName
17
18    num getHourlyWage()
19    return hourlyWage
20
21    num getWeeklyPay()
22    return weeklyPay
23
24    void calculateWeeklyPay()
25        num WORK_WEEK_HOURS = 40
26        weeklyPay = hourlyWage * WORK_WEEK_HOURS
27    return
28 endClass
```

Figure 10-1 Pseudocode for Employee class

```
 1 // Employee class
 2 public class Employee
 3 {
 4     private String lastName;
 5     private double hourlyWage;
 6     private double weeklyPay;
 7
 8     public void setLastName(String name)
 9     {
10         lastName = name;
11         return;
12     }
13
14     public void setHourlyWage(double wage)
15     {
16         hourlyWage = wage;
17         calculateWeeklyPay();
18         return;
19     }
20
21     public String getLastName()
22     {
23         return lastName;
24     }
25
26     public double getHourlyWage()
27     {
28         return hourlyWage;
29     }
30
31     public double getWeeklyPay()
32     {
33         return weeklyPay;
34     }
35
36     private void calculateWeeklyPay()
37     {
38         final int WORK_WEEK_HOURS = 40;
39         weeklyPay = hourlyWage * WORK_WEEK_HOURS;
40         return;
41     }
42 } // End Employee class
```

Figure 10-2 Employee class implemented in Java

Looking at the pseudocode in Figure 10-1, you see that you begin creating a class by specifying that it is a class. In the Java code in Figure 10-2, line 1 is a comment. This is followed by the class declaration for the Employee class on line 2. The class declaration begins with the keyword, public, which allows this class to be used in programs, followed by the keyword, class, which specifies that what follows is a Java class. The opening curly brace on line 3 and the closing curly brace on line 42 mark the beginning and the end of the class.

Adding Attributes to a Class

The next step is to define the attributes (data) that are included in the `Employee` class. As shown on lines 2, 3, and 4 of the pseudocode in Figure 10-1, there are three attributes in this pseudocode class, `string lastName`, `num hourlyWage`, and `num weeklyPay`.

Lines 4, 5, and 6 in Figure 10-2 include these attributes in the Java version of the `Employee` class. Notice in the Java code that `hourlyWage` and `weeklyPay` are defined using the `double` data type, and `lastName` is defined as a `String`. Also, notice that all three attributes are `private`. As explained in *Programming Logic and Design, Sixth Edition*, this means the data cannot be accessed by any method that is not part of the class. Programs that use the `Employee` class must use the methods that are part of the class to access private data.

Adding Methods to a Class

The next step is to add methods to the `Employee` class. The pseudocode versions of these methods, shown on lines 6 through 27 in Figure 10-1, are nonstatic methods. As you learned in Chapter 10 of *Programming Logic and Design, Sixth Edition*, **nonstatic methods** are methods that are meant to be used with an object created from a class. In other words, to use these methods, we must create an object of the `Employee` class first and then use that object to invoke (or call) the method.

The code shown in Figure 10-2 shows how to include methods in the `Employee` class using Java. We will start the discussion with the set methods. You learned in *Programming Logic and Design, Sixth Edition* that **set methods** are those whose purpose is to set the values of attributes (data fields) within the class. There are three data fields in the `Employee` class, but we will only add two set methods, `setLastName()` and `setHourlyWage()`. We will not add a `setWeeklyPay()` method, because the `weeklyPay` data field will be set by the `setHourlyWage()` method. The `setHourlyWage()` method uses another method, `calculateWeeklyPay()`, to accomplish this.

The two set methods, `setLastName()` shown on lines 8 through 12 in Figure 10-2, and `setHourlyWage()` shown on lines 14 through 19, are declared using the keyword `public`. This means that programs may use these methods to gain access to the private data. The `calculateWeeklyPay()` method, shown on lines 36 through

41 in Figure 10-2, is `private`, which means it must be called from within another method that already belongs to the class. In the `Employee` class, the `calculateWeeklyPay()` method is called from the `setHourlyWage()` method (line 17), which ensures that the class retains full control over when and how the `calculateWeeklyPay()` method is used.

The `setLastName()` method (lines 8 through 12) accepts one argument, `String name`, that is assigned to the private attribute, `lastName`. This sets the value of `lastName`. The `setLastName()` method is a `void` method—that is, it returns nothing.

The `setHourlyWage()` method (lines 14 through 19) accepts one argument, `double wage`, that is assigned to the private attribute, `hourlyWage`. This sets the value of `hourlyWage`. Next, it calls the `private` method, `calculateWeeklyPay()`. The `calculateWeeklyPay()` method does not accept arguments. Within the method, on line 38, a constant, `final int WORK_WEEK_HOURS`, is declared and initialized with the value 40. The `calculateWeeklyPay()` method then calculates weekly pay (line 39) by multiplying the private attribute, `hourlyWage`, by `WORK_WEEK_HOURS`. The result is assigned to the private attribute, `weeklyPay`. The `setHourlyWage()` method and the `calculateWeeklyPay()` method are `void` methods, which means they return nothing.

The final step in creating the `Employee` class is adding the get methods. **Get methods** are methods that return a value to the program using the class. The pseudocode in Figure 10-1 includes three get methods, `getLastName()` on lines 15 and 16, `getHourlyWage()` on lines 18 and 19, and `getWeeklyPay()` on lines 21 and 22. Lines 21 through 34 in Figure 10-2 illustrate the Java version of the get methods in the `Employee` class.

The three get methods are `public` methods and accept no arguments. The `getLastName()` method, shown on lines 21 through 24, returns a `String`, which is the value of the private attribute, `lastName`. The `getHourlyWage()` method, shown on lines 26 through 29, returns a `double`, which is the value of the private attribute, `hourlyWage`, and the `getWeeklyPay()` method, shown on lines 31 through 34, also returns a `double`, which is the value of the private attribute, `weeklyPay`.

The `Employee` class is now complete and may be used in a Java program. The `Employee` class does not contain a `main()` method because it is not an application but rather a class that an application may now use to instantiate objects.

The completed `Employee` class is included in the student files provided for this book in a file named `Employee.java`.

Figure 10-3 illustrates a program named Employee Wages that uses the `Employee` class.

```
1 // This program uses the programmer-defined Employee class.
2
3 public class EmployeeWages
4 {
5     public static void main(String args[])
6     {
7         final double LOW = 9.00;
8         final double HIGH = 14.65;
9         // Instantiate an Employee object
10        Employee myGardener = new Employee();
11
12        // Use the get and set methods
13        myGardener.setLastName("Greene");
14        myGardener.setHourlyWage(LOW);
15        System.out.println("My gardener makes " +
16                myGardener.getWeeklyPay() + " per week.");
17
18        // Use the get and set methods
19        myGardener.setHourlyWage(HIGH);
20        System.out.println("My gardener makes " +
21                myGardener.getWeeklyPay() + " per week.");
22        System.exit(0);
23    }
24 }
```

Figure 10-3   Employee Wages program that uses the `Employee` class

As shown in Figure 10-3, the Employee Wages program begins with a comment on line 1, followed by the creation of a class named `EmployeeWages` on line 3. This class contains a `main()` method that begins on line 5. A `main()` method must be written in this class because it is an application. As in other programs you have seen throughout this book, the `main()` method header includes the keyword `static`. As you learned in Chapter 10 of *Programming Logic and Design, Sixth Edition*, **static methods** are those for which no object needs to exist. This means that you do not need to create a `EmployeeWages` object in order to call the `main()` method. On lines 7 and 8 within the `main()` method, two constants, `LOW` and `HIGH`, are declared and initialized. Next, on line 10, an `Employee` object (an instance of the `Employee` class) is created with the following statement:

```
Employee myGardener = new Employee();
```

In Java, a statement that creates a new object consists of the class name followed by the object's name. In the preceding example, the class is `Employee`, and the name of the object is `myGardener`. Next comes the assignment operator, followed by the `new` keyword and the name of a constructor you want to use to create the object.

You used the `new` keyword to instantiate `FileReader` and `FileWriter` objects in Chapter 7 of this book.

As you learned in *Programming Logic and Design, Sixth Edition*, a
constructor is a method that creates an object. You also learned that you
can use a prewritten **default constructor**, which is a constructor that
expects no arguments and is created automatically by the compiler for
every class you write. The `Employee()` constructor used in the Employee
Wages program is an example of a prewritten default constructor.

Constructors always have the same name as the class and are always written with no return value—not even `void`.

187

Once the `myGardener` object is created, we can use `myGardener` to
invoke the set methods to set the value of `lastName` to "Greene" and
the `hourlyWage` to `LOW`. The syntax used is shown in the following
code sample.

```
myGardener.setLastName("Greene");
myGardener.setHourlyWage(LOW);
```

This is the syntax used to invoke a method with an instance (an
object) of a class.

You can also write your own constructors. You will learn more about additional constructors in future Java courses.

On lines 15 and 16 in Figure 10-3, the program then prints "My
gardener makes" (a string constant) followed by the return value of
`myGardener.getWeeklyPay()`, followed by the string constant " per
week". Here, the `myGardener` object is used again—this time to invoke
the `getWeeklyPay()` method.

On line 19, `myGardener` invokes the set method, `setHourlyWage()`,
to set a new value for `hourlyWage`. This time `hourlyWage` is set
to `HIGH`. The program then prints (lines 20 and 21) "My gardener makes" (a string constant) followed by the return value of
`myGardener.getWeeklyPay()`, followed by the string constant " per
week." The `System.exit(0);` statement on line 22 ends the program.
The output from this program is shown in Figure 10-4.

Notice the syntax, `objectName.methodName`, in which the name of the object is separated from the name of the method by a dot, which is actually a period.

Figure 10-4 Output from the Employee Wages program

You will find the completed program in a file named
`EmployeeWages.java` included with the student files for this book.

Exercise 10-1: Creating a Programmer-Defined Class in Java

In this exercise, you use what you have learned about creating and
using a programmer-defined class. Study the following code, and then
answer Questions 1–4.

```
class Circle
{
   private double radius;    // Radius of this circle
   final double PI = 3.14159;
   public void setRadius(double rad)
   {
      radius = rad;
   }
   public double getRadius()
   {
      return radius;
   }
   public double calculateCircumference()
   {
      return (2 * PI * radius);
   }
   public double calculateArea()
   {
      return(PI * radius * radius);
   }
} // End of Circle class
```

In this exercise, assume that a Circle object named myCircle has been created in a program that uses the Circle class, and radius is given a value as shown in the following code.

```
Circle myCircle = new Circle();
myCircle.setRadius(6.0);
```

1. What is the output when the following line of Java code executes?

   ```
   System.out.println("The circumference is : " +
           myCircle.calculateCircumference());
   ```

   _____

2. Is the following a legal Java statement? Why or why not?

   ```
   System.out.println("The area is : " + calculateArea());
   ```

   _____

3. Consider the following Java code. What is the value stored in the myCircle object's attribute named radius?

   ```
   myCircle.setRadius(8.0);
   ```

   _____

4. Write the Java code that will assign the circumference of myCircle to a double variable named circumference2.

   _____

LAB 10.1   Creating a Class in Java

In this lab, you will create a programmer-defined class and then use it in a Java program. The program should create two `Rectangle` objects and find their area and perimeter. Use the `Circle` class that you worked with in Exercise 10-1 as a guide.

1. Open the class file named `Rectangle.java` using Notepad or the text editor of your choice.

2. In the `Rectangle` class, create two private attributes named `length` and `width`. Both `length` and `width` should be data type `double`.

3. Write `public` set methods to set the values for `length` and `width`.

4. Write `public` get methods to retrieve the values for `length` and `width`.

5. Write a `public calculateArea()` method and a `public calculatePerimeter()` method to calculate and return the area of the rectangle and the perimeter of the rectangle.

6. Save this class file, `Rectangle.java`, in a directory of your choice, and then open the file named `MyRectangleClassProgram.java`.

7. In the `MyRectangleClassProgram` class, create two `Rectangle` objects named `rectangle1` and `rectangle2` using the default constructor as you saw in `EmployeeWages.java`.

8. Set the length of `rectangle1` to 5.0 and the width to 3.0. Set the length of `rectangle2` to 7.0 and the width to 5.0.

9. Print the value of `rectangle1`'s perimeter and area, and then print the value of `rectangle2`'s perimeter and area.

10. Save `MyRectangleClassProgram.java` in the same directory as `Rectangle.java`.

11. Compile the source code file `MyRectangleClassProgram.java`.

12. Execute the program.

13. Record the output below.

_____

_____

Creating a Graphical User Interface (GUI)

You should do the exercises and labs in this section after you have finished Chapter 12 in *Programming Logic and Design, Sixth Edition*, which discusses creating a **Graphical User Interface** (GUI). To review briefly, a GUI allows users to interact with programs by using a mouse to point, drag, or click. GUI programs are referred to as **event-driven** or **event-based** because this type of program responds to user-initiated events, such as a mouse click. Within a GUI program, an **event listener** waits for an event to occur and then responds to it. An event listener is actually a method that contains Java code that executes when a particular event occurs. For example, when a user of a GUI program clicks a button, an event occurs. In response to the event, the event listener (a method) that is written as part of the GUI program executes.

In order to create full-blown, event-driven programs that make use of a graphical user interface, you need to learn more about Java than is included in this book. In this section, you will learn to use just a few of the many graphical user interface Components that are included in the JDK, such as a button, a label, and a frame. You will also learn to write event listeners that respond to specific user actions, such as clicking.

The Java program shown in Figure 10-5 creates the graphical user interface shown in Figure 10-6. This GUI is made up of a frame, a panel, some buttons, and some labels. When the program executes, the user can click buttons to change the color of a button or the background color of the panel. You will learn about buttons, labels, frames, and panels in the following sections.

```
1 import javax.swing.*;
2 import java.awt.*;
3 import java.awt.event.*;
4
5 class GuiDemo
6 {
7     JPanel panel;
8
9     GuiDemo()
10    {
11        JLabel redLabel = new JLabel("Click to change color");
12        JLabel blueLabel =
13                new JLabel("Click to change color");
14        JLabel backLabel =
15                new JLabel("Click to change background color");
16
```

Figure 10-5   Java program that uses a Graphical User Interface (GUI) *(continues)*

(continued)

```
17        final JButton redButton = new JButton("Red");
18        redButton.addActionListener(new ActionListener(){
19            public void actionPerformed(ActionEvent e){
20                redButton.setBackground(Color.RED);
21            }
22        });
23        final JButton blueButton = new JButton("Blue");
24        blueButton.addActionListener(new ActionListener(){
25            public void actionPerformed(ActionEvent e){
26                blueButton.setBackground(Color.BLUE);
27            }
28        });
29        final JButton backButton = new JButton("Background");
30        backButton.addActionListener(new ActionListener(){
31            public void actionPerformed(ActionEvent e){
32                panel.setBackground(Color.GREEN);
33            }
34        });
35
36        panel = new JPanel();
37
38        panel.add(redLabel);
39        panel.add(redButton);
40
41        panel.add(blueLabel);
42        panel.add(blueButton);
43
44        panel.add(backLabel);
45        panel.add(backButton);
46    }
47
48    public static void main(String args[])
49    {
50        GuiDemo demo = new GuiDemo();
51        JFrame frame = new JFrame("GUI Demo");
52        frame.setDefaultCloseOperation(JFrame.EXIT_ON_CLOSE);
53
54        frame.setContentPane(demo.panel);
55        frame.pack();
56        frame.setVisible(true);
57    }
58 }
```

Figure 10-5   Java program that uses a Graphical User Interface (GUI)

Figure 10-6   Graphical User Interface created by `GuiDemo.java`

In Figure 10-5, lines 1, 2, and 3 are `import` statements that import packages. You learned about `import` statements in Chapter 2 of this book. Remember that a **package** is a group of related classes. The classes used in this program are part of the packages named `javax.swing`, `java.awt`, and `java.awt.event`. When you **import** a class, a program then has access to the methods that are part of that class. The `javax.swing` package contains components such as the `JButton` class. The `java.awt` package contains component classes as well as other graphics classes, such as the `Color` class. The `java.awt.event` package contains classes that we can use to write event listeners that respond to events.

Line 5 in Figure 10-5 begins the class named `GuiDemo`. The first statement (line 7) in the `GuiDemo` class uses the `JPanel` class to create a reference to a `JPanel` object named `panel`. The reference is not itself a `JPanel` object, but merely a location in memory where the address of an actual `JPanel` object will be stored later in the program. A **JPanel** is a Java component that is considered a `Container`. In Java, a **Container** is a component that is used to hold or organize other components. In this program, the `JPanel` is used to hold buttons and labels.

Writing a Constructor

Lines 9 through 46 of Figure 10-5 include a method named `GuiDemo()`. You know this method is a constructor because it has the same name as the class. This constructor expects no arguments and will execute when a `GuiDemo` object is created. Within the `GuiDemo()` constructor (lines 11 through 15), we create three `JLabel` objects named `redLabel`, `blueLabel`, and `backLabel` as:

```
JLabel redLabel = new JLabel("Click to change color");
JLabel blueLabel =
       new JLabel("Click to change color");
JLabel backLabel =
       new JLabel("Click to change background color");
```

In Java, a `JLabel` is used to display a single line of read-only text. **Read-only** means that the user cannot change the text that is displayed. In this example, the interface displays two instances of read-only text: "Click to change color" and "Click to change background color".

The next section of code is rather complicated:

```
final JButton redButton = new JButton("Red");
redButton.addActionListener(new ActionListener(){
    public void actionPerformed(ActionEvent e){
         redButton.setBackground(Color.RED);
    }
```

```
});
final JButton blueButton = new JButton("Blue");
blueButton.addActionListener(new ActionListener(){
    public void actionPerformed(ActionEvent e){
        blueButton.setBackground(Color.BLUE);
    }
});
final JButton backButton = new JButton("Background");
backButton.addActionListener(new ActionListener(){
    public void actionPerformed(ActionEvent e){
        panel.setBackground(Color.GREEN);
    }
});
```

This code (lines 17 through 34 in Figure 10-5) creates JButton objects and attaches event listener methods to the JButtons. The following three lines of code (lines 17, 23, and 29) create three JButton objects known as push buttons. When a user clicks (pushes) a JButton, an event occurs that causes something to happen in the program. In this program, clicking the redButton causes it to turn red, clicking the blueButton causes it to turn blue, and clicking the backButton causes the background color of the JPanel to turn green. The string constants within the parentheses cause the text "Red", "Blue", or "Background" to be displayed on the JButtons.

In Java, local variables, such as JButtons, must be declared **final** to be used in an anonymous inner class, which is discussed next.

```
final JButton redButton = new JButton("Red");
final JButton blueButton = new JButton("Blue");
final JButton backButton = new JButton("Background");
```

Next, let's look at the event handlers. The following code (lines 18 through 22) adds an event handler to the JButton named redButton:

```
redButton.addActionListener(new ActionListener(){
    public void actionPerformed(ActionEvent e){
        redButton.setBackground(Color.RED);
    }
});
```

The redButton object invokes the addActionListener() method (line 18) and passes a new ActionListener object as a parameter. In Java, JButton objects generate Action Events when they are clicked and require an event listener to handle the Action Event. The event listener for Action Events is called an ActionListener. Therefore, the redButton requires an ActionListener. To add the ActionListener to the redButton, we need to create a new ActionListener object. This we accomplish by creating an **anonymous inner class**, which is a class that does not have a name and that is nested within another class.

The program has access to the addActionListener() method and ActionEvent objects because we imported the java.awt.event package.

194

Within this inner class, we need to write one method, `public void actionPerformed(ActionEvent e)`. The `actionPerformed()` method must be written to accept one parameter, an `ActionEvent` object, which, in this program, is named `e`.

This method contains code that instructs the program what action to take when the user clicks the `redButton`. The code required for this program (line 20) is shown in the following example.

```
redButton.setBackground(Color.RED);
```

The `redButton` object invokes the `setBackground(Color.RED)` method and passes `Color.RED` as an argument. This method changes the color of the `redButton` object to the color passed to it. In this case, the color is red.

You have access to the `setBackground()` method because it is contained in the `JButton` class, which is part of the `javax.swing` package you imported.

You have access to the `Color` class because you imported the `java.awt` package. Several attributes are defined in the `Color` class, including RED, BLUE, and GREEN.

Lines 23 through 28 add an `ActionListener` to the `JButton` named `blueButton` to change its color to `Color.BLUE` when it is clicked. Similarly, lines 29 through 34 add an `ActionListener` to the `JButton` named `backButton` to change the color of the `JPanel` named `panel` to `Color.GREEN` when it is clicked.

Line 36 creates a `JPanel` object and assigns its reference (memory address) to `panel`. Lines 38 through 45 use `panel` (the `JPanel` object) to invoke the `add()` method. The `add()` method is used to add the `JLabels` and `JButtons` to the `JPanel` container. You are now finished writing the `GuiDemo()` constructor.

Writing the `main()` Method

As shown in Figure 10-5, the `main()` method is included in the `GuiDemo` class.

Remember, the `main()` method is the first method called when a program executes.

The first line of code (line 50) in the `main()` method, `GuiDemo demo = new GuiDemo();`, is responsible for creating a new `GuiDemo` object named `demo`. This line causes the `GuiDemo()` constructor to be called. As you saw previously, the `GuiDemo()` constructor creates the graphical user interface by adding `JLabels` and `JButtons` to a `JPanel`. It also assigns `ActionListeners` to the `JButtons`.

The next step is to create a `JFrame` object named `frame` (line 51), as follows:

```
JFrame frame = new JFrame("GUI Demo");
```

A JFrame is a Window that can have a border, a title bar, and a menu bar. In this example, the string constant "GUI Demo" (in parentheses) is specified as the title for the JFrame title bar.

The next line of code (line 52),

```
frame.setDefaultCloseOperation(JFrame.EXIT_ON_CLOSE);
```

is a shortcut technique for adding an event handler to a JFrame. It causes the JFrame window to close when the user clicks the X button on the title bar.

The syntax for accessing panel (the name of the JPanel) is demo.panel because panel is a member of the GuiDemo object named demo.

The last three lines in the main() method (lines 54, 55, and 56) look like this:

```
frame.setContentPane(demo.panel);
frame.pack();
frame.setVisible(true);
```

The **ContentPane** is the container to which you add Components such as JButtons and JLabels. In this case, we want to use JPanel as a ContentPane. To specify this, we pass the name of the JPanel (in this case, demo.panel) to the setContentPane() method.

You might wonder why you would want to create a JFrame that you cannot see. Many Java programs consist of multiple JFrames that are displayed to the user at different times.

The method named pack() causes the JFrame to be sized to fit the size of the Components that have been added to it. The method named setVisible() allows users to see the JFrame if it receives true as an argument. Passing false to the setVisible() method keeps the JFrame from being seen.

The Gui Demo program is now complete. The program is stored in a file named GuiDemo.java along with the other student files for this book. You should compile the program and then execute it to see the JButtons or the JPanel change color when you click the buttons.

Exercise 10-2: Creating a Graphical User Interface in Java

In this exercise, you use what you have learned about creating a graphical user interface to answer Questions 1–4.

1. Write the Java statement that creates a JPanel named myPanel.

2. Write the Java statement that creates a JButton named myButton. The JButton should include the text "OK".

3. Write the Java statement that adds myButton to the JPanel named myPanel.

_____

4. Write the Java statement that changes the color of myButton to orange.

_____

LAB 10.2 Creating a Graphical User Interface in Java

In this lab, you create a graphical user interface in a partially completed Java program. The program should create two JButtons. Display the text "Yes" on one of the JButtons, and display the text "No" on the other JButton. You should also create three JLabels. Display the text "Do you like GUI programming? Vote Yes or No." on one of the JLabels. Display the text "Click here to vote Yes" on another JLabel, and display the text "Click here to vote No" on the third JLabel. Also, add event handlers that cause the background color of the JPanel to change to yellow if a user votes "Yes" and to red if a user votes "No". Use the GuiDemo class discussed in this section as a guide.

1. Open the file named JavaQuiz.java using Notepad or the text editor of your choice.

2. Create the three JLabels named labelYes, labelNo, and labelQuestion with the text described above.

3. Create two JButtons named buttonYes and buttonNo with the text described above.

4. Create a JPanel named myPanel.

5. Save the file, JavaQuiz.java, in a directory of your choice.

6. Compile the file JavaQuiz.java.

7. Execute the program.

Index

198

204